Travels On The Private Zodiac

Reflections on Jewish Life, Ritual, and Spirituality

Martin Samuel Cohen

MOONSTONE PRESS

Cover art: Courtesy Jewish Museum/Art Resource, NY. Sukkah Decoration. Trieste, c.1775, by Israel David Luzzato (1746-1806). Ink and watercolor on paper. 20 x 15½ in. The H. Ephraim and Mordecai Benguiat Family Collection, S0066550   S256   Color Transp.

Cover design and imaging by Ceneda Creative Inc., Toronto. Author photograph by Rozelle Sieff. Typesetting and design by The Writer-in-Residence, London. Printed and bound in Canada by Kromar Printing Ltd.,Winnipeg.

Moonstone Press gratefully acknowledges the financial assistance of the Ontario Arts Council, the Canada Council, and the Heritage Cultures and Languages Program, Department of Canadian Heritage.

Canadian Cataloguing in Publication Data

Cohen, Martin Samuel, 1953-
    Travels on the private zodiac: reflections on Jewish life, ritual and spirituality

ISBN 0-920259-56-1

1. Jewish way of life. 2. Judaism — Customs and practice. I. Title.

BM723.C65 1995   296.7   C95-931768-6

Moonstone Press
167 Delaware St.
London, Ontario
Canada N5Z 2N6

For Joseph Rispublik, Yefim Kharkover
Adolphus Gottesman, Wilhelm Kaufmann,
Seymour Schmink, Hans-Joachim Schwartz,
Isadore Zobel, Maurice Lipshitz,
Tzvi Hirsch Slonim, Yitzchak Tarnover,
Elimelech Weissbrot, Eli Adam Lookstein,
Robert Snitkoff, Barbara Snitkoff,
Adam Irrwitz, Levi Mauskopf,
Richard Rosenkrantz
and
Aaron Menachem Isaac Rakman

CONTENTS

*L*ong ago, there was a magic kingdom so vast that there was a separate magic forest in it for each individual citizen to explore and enjoy. And the magic of these forests lay in this: the paths in each single forest were all magically interconnected so that no matter how far in any one direction a citizen might absent-mindedly walk, the path he was travelling eventually brought him to the destination he had had in mind upon entering the forest. However, since no wanderer ever met another in the forest that was designated for his sole use, this fact went unnoticed and its implications unconsidered for many generations. Eventually, of course, the citizenry grew so large that this arrangement could no longer be continued and two citizens were assigned the same magic forest in which to wander. As time passed, the numbers increased until each forest became crowded with wanderers and hikers. Although the magic nature of the forest stopped once the citizens began to ponder the impossible physics involved in a forest in which all the paths led automatically to the precise spot each individual wanderer was seeking on any particular visit, some vestigial remnant of the ancient wonder lingered on in this: the paths that had led those who trod them to their desired destinations now only led those who wandered them deeper and deeper into the primeval forest. As there were now no paths out at all, the citizenry began to diminish as countless numbers of wanderers disappeared into the kingdom's vast forests never to be heard from again. When the citizenry was finally shrunk down to its original size, the kingdom returned to its former practice of assigning each individual citizen his or her own forest to explore. The magic returned immediately, but, of course, no one noticed ...

— *Elimelech Weissbrot*

PREFACE

The men and woman to whom this book is dedicated are the rabbis who populate the pages of my novels, both the one which has been published and those which circulate privately. I am often asked if these rabbis, with all their deformities, peccadilloes, weaknesses and occasional strengths represent some sort of psychic projection of my own rabbinic persona onto the pages of my own books and this might well be the right place to answer that question with a definitive "maybe." I am indeed what I write, as is any serious author. But as much as it may be true that I have created these rabbinic colleagues to serve the fictitious congregations in my books, as time has passed, it is also somewhat true that they, as a group, have also created the rabbi I myself have become. As a result, I am both these rabbis' creator and their creation, both the caster of their shadows and the rabbinic amalgam of the fictitious shadows they somehow manage to cast. I am, therefore, in their debt at least to the extent that they are in mine, and possibly more so. To them all, my sincere gratitude.

The essays contained in this book are all parts of a larger attempt to explain the attraction Judaism holds for me and I offer them to the reading public in the hope that they will demonstrate the plausibility of understanding Judaism in a way that is traditional without being fundamentalist, liberal without being naive, intellectual without being pedantic and spiritual without being mercenary, self-serving or vacuous. I believe that the faith and beliefs that motivate and generate Jewish life can indeed be all those things and, if this book manages to convince its readers that I am right to think so, then it will have been well worth the effort it has taken me to produce it.

About half of these essays were written over many years and in many places, but the other half were written in the spring of 1993 while I had the privilege of being the first Daniel Jeremy Silver fellow at Harvard University. To the administrators and benefactors of the trust, I extend my sincerest thanks, as I do to the members and directors of the Beth Tikvah Congregation in Richmond, British Columbia, who made it possible for me to leave my congregational duties for six months in order to work and write at Harvard. The Silver fellowship exists in the hope that the present distinction the Jewish world seems bent on making between serious scholars and working congregational rabbis become obliterated and, eventually, archaic; it is my hope that this book will help prove that the ideal forum for the development of Jewish ideas is indeed the congregational setting. That was Rabbi Silver's dream and it is mine as well.

M.S.C.
Richmond, British Columbia
1995

I. Life Inside the Story

There was a time not very long ago when the worst thing you could say about a religious ritual was that it was "primitive". There was something about that word that said it all — primitive rituals were superstitious, ritualistic acts better suited to the naked natives in the pages of National Geographic than to the kind of genteel, sophisticated people you find gathering for genteel, sophisticated religious activities in your average congregation. People want to think of their own religion, whatever it is, as advanced and enlightened, the kind of faith that is willing to jettison whatever baggage it may have inadvertently inherited from its unenlightened, pre-advanced ancestors in favour of rituals and rites that have their roots in poetry rather than in magic and which serve as pleasant adornments to faith rather than as tools designed to have any real effect on reality one way or the other.

It all sounds grand, but the problem is that Judaism is deeply ritualistic in its orientation and the rituals Judaism considers the most important are mostly all ones that are not only primitive, but deeply, unalterably so. My dictionary says that "primitive" things are crude, simple, rough, uncivilized, primary and basic, things characteristic or imitative of the earliest times or ages. And so indeed are our earliest Jewish rituals primary, basic things, practices designed to allow the trappings of the specific culture in which an individual Jew might live to fall away and leave that Jew in a state of deep identification with the Jews of all places and all generations by performing the same act they themselves performed as a means of stepping across the outer perimeter into the sacred space in which every individual Jew dwells alone with God.

But there's more to it than that. The primitive nature of our rituals is not only an accident of history with which we must live, but is actually what makes them so attractive to us. Or at least to me.

There's something peculiar about all Jewish rituals and specifically about the way they intersect with the myths that inspire and justify them. Every nation, after all, has its myths and its rituals. In some societies, these are preserved as fairly separate domains, while in other cultures they are related to each other formally, even if sometimes a bit artificially.

The relationship between ritual and myth in Judaism is different and, in some ways, unique. We don't merely tell our stories, we climb into them and live them out as though we were actors in a life-long ritual drama designed to develop some specific aspect of our faith from a state of dormancy to its fullest flower. Scripture wishes us to believe that God is the Creator of the world. Is that simple to believe? Does the world appear entirely as if it were made by a benevolent, loving Deity? It does not. And so we start with a story, the story told in the first chapter of the Bible. It's a lovely story, a charming story, a naive story told by ancient people to ancient people to make one single point: that God made the world. Is it true? I don't suppose I really know, but even if I *were* certain that God couldn't possibly have made the world in six days, it wouldn't make much difference because the alleged truth of the story isn't what makes it appealing or important to me in the first place.

What *is* important is for a people to respond to something deep within its national soul that yearns to love God. Where it comes from, I don't know. Whether it is uniquely Jewish or part of the common spiritual heritage of all mankind, I also don't know. But whether it is unique to us or shared with others, it is still a profound part of who we are and why we endure. But love is not something that can exist in the absence of intimate knowledge; indeed, what is love if not the name we give to a relationship between two individuals founded on knowledge so intimate that it differs qualitatively from friendship or acquaintanceship or any other kind of relationship that we mortals experience? And so we set out in pursuit of love by training ourselves in the knowledge of God, by weaving a blanket of faith one thread at a time.

We wish to know God as the Creator of the world, so we construct a story, sanctify its detail and then, instead of merely telling the tale to each other, we live within the story, actually acting out the six days of creation and one day of rest not once or twice, but every week of our lives. And, as the years and decades pass and the rhythm of this particular ritual becomes internalized, we do indeed find ourselves seeing God as the Creator of the world. This is what is primitive about the ritual — it doesn't exist to *remind* us that God created the world, but to create the context in which we can internalize such an outlandish, unlikely piece of theological dogma and eventually, almost magically, come to believe it.

Every one of the commandments and all of the rituals of Biblical and post-Biblical Judaism exist to weave single threads in this worn blanket of faith in which we wish to wrap ourselves. We eat matzah and bitter herbs at Passover not merely as a spur to recollecting the exodus from Egypt, but as part of an elaborate year-long cycle of events that allows us actually to live inside the story of that exodus and, in so doing, to internalize the concept of God as the source of liberation from whatever it might be that enslaves any of us. We observe our complex dietary laws not because there's something *wrong* with eating eels or owls, but because we wish to train ourselves to behave like grateful guests in God's world, guests who politely eat what their Host is serving despite knowing full well that the choices for that evening's menu were made arbitrarily and are thus utterly devoid of deep meaning or ulterior significance. We say our prayers not because God needs to hear the praise of mortals, whatever that would mean, but because we wish to train ourselves to acknowledge God as the author of dialogue and dialectic, the Other who hears and who listens, the Thou to every I and the I to every thou.

Some of our rituals have not weathered the centuries well and have been quietly dropped. Others have come into existence as responses to specific gaps in the Scriptural programme. Some have become obscure, while the meaning of others remains crystal clear, that clarity only the better served by the uncompromising primitiveness of the specific ritual involved. When we take a knife in hand and carve the sign of the covenant into the flesh of every newborn boy, we are not merely *saying* that we feel the vagaries and vicissitudes of Jewish history to be the ebb and flow of a covenantal relationship between God and Israel that has endured for millennia, we are living inside that belief by guaranteeing that the Jewish generation our own children will produce will be created under the same sign of the covenant beneath which they themselves were made.

Nothing could be more primitive than circumcision, but neither could any ritual be more satisfying or more direct or more in tune with the way in which human beings come to have faith in God. So as the dictionary says is primitive, so is my Judaism: crude, simple, rough, uncivilized, primary and basic. And as spiritually effective as it is blunt, frank and unadorned.

2. Time Off and Out

S habbat — the Jewish Sabbath — must seem absolutely awful from the outside looking in. All those rules restricting even the most off-hand activity — no writing, no shopping, no cooking, no smoking, no carrying — can't possibly make Shabbat sound too appealing to anyone trying to analyze the institution in a dispassionate, impartial way.

And, at least in this case, there's something to say for appearances. The Sabbath laws *are* restrictive and difficult to observe. There's no question that there have been many times when I don't think my spiritual life would have been seriously damaged by making a piece of toast to go along with my Saturday afternoon tea. (We keep an electric urn of hot water switched on from Friday afternoon to Saturday night so we don't actually have to boil the water we use to make the tea.) And there have been times when it would have been pleasant, even relaxing, to curl up in bed with a pen and pad of paper and write a letter to a friend to whom I've been meaning to write for a while. I don't drive on Shabbat either, not even to and from synagogue, which means that I get wet when it's raining and I get snowed on when it snows. It means that I was a sitting duck for the juvenile delinquents who ran after me one Friday night last year screaming "Heil Hitler" as I walked home from synagogue. And it means that I can't go anywhere that's not a reasonable walk from my home for twenty-five whole hours. (Shabbat begins a little more than a quarter hour before sundown on Friday and ends about three quarters of an hour after sundown on Saturday.)

And we're pretty *liberal* in our observance. Joan and I have friends who keep boxes of Kleenex in their bathrooms because they won't rip sheets of toilet paper on Shabbat. And we have others who hang their keys from their belt buckles when they go out on the Sabbath because they feel that even having a key in one's jacket pocket is a contravention of the Sabbath laws they are trying to live by. Then there was my father's Auntie Tsirel who used to open the tap with her elbow on Saturdays, lest she be accused (by whom?) of transporting water from the reservoir to her sink on Shabbat. (Why opening the tap with her elbow made this less of a problem was a secret Auntie Tsirel took with her to the grave. Possibly it has something to do with the rabbinic idea that illicit actions are only truly forbidden when performed in the normal way, but I somehow doubt that was her reasoning. If I could, I'd ask.)

Are we having fun yet? Now, it must seem almost impossible to imagine, but observing Shabbat is the high point of my week. I am neither a masochist nor a maniac and neither am I particularly fanatic in my approach either to Scripture or to Jewish law. I don't think of myself as a zealot — far from it — and yet the truth is that Sabbath observance has enormously enhanced the quality of my life. And, in the larger picture of things, doing without toast is worth it.

The basic idea is that there are two things we all do in our lives: work and not work. In the non-Jewish world, work is considered what you get paid by someone to do. You go to work and you do whatever it is you get paid to do and then, when you're through doing it, you go home and you don't do it. As far as I can tell, that's the basic way most people define work — and everything else is considered not working. So making toast isn't working and picking up the dry cleaning isn't working and doing the marketing isn't working either. Neither is doing your tax returns or driving your kids around to *their* various activities or any of the other stuff people do when they're not at work. In fact, nothing is work except what you do at the office or at the job site or in your store or, if you're a cowboy, out on the range.

Jews have a different approach. To us, everything is work. Shlepping around after your children is work. Ironing is work. Taking the dog to the vet is work. Doing your job is *certainly* work also, but it isn't that different from the rest of your chores except that you get paid for it — which, if anything, makes it *less* arduous and irritating than your unremunerated tasks. Now this is the genius of Judaism: if all that stuff is work, then you still get your Sabbath day for leisure pursuits. (The Gentile world gets its weekends off too, but they're too busy picking up their dry cleaning and mowing their lawns to get too much pleasure out of it.)

And of what does this leisure consist? We sit. We think. We say our prayers. We eat as a family. We drink wine. We sing. We drink tea and discuss Things That Count. We make love. We sleep in. We go to synagogue and hear Scripture read to us. We nap. We commune with our families and our friends and with ourselves. We play with our children. We rest.

Now, we also have our chores to do. But we think of them as work and we do them during the work week. Somehow, it all gets fit in and that leaves time over for Shabbat activities — and *that's* leisure. That's rest. That's rejuvenation and restoration. That's why I like Shabbat so much — because it is the only time all week when I can sit for a few minutes and not feel guilty about the fact that I *should* be doing something else. (I probably *should* be doing something else, only I don't feel guilty about it. In fact, I feel great about it. Even noble.)

In ancient times, the average citizen went to sleep at sundown and got up at sunup. But on Friday evenings, when the rituals welcoming the arrival of Shabbat must be performed after evening falls, it was customary for even the poorest Jewish family to find the wherewithal to purchase enough oil to light their homes after sundown. Even though those days are long gone and nobody goes to sleep with the sun anymore, we have sanctified what was our ancestors' practice of necessity and we too light Sabbath lamps in our homes. Hardly anyone uses oil anymore, but the Sabbath candles have taken over as the best-known symbol of Shabbat observance.

At our house, my wife lights her Shabbat candles in candlesticks that we bought in Jerusalem shortly before our first son was born. So there I am, king of my tiny castle, bathed in the yellow light of our

Jerusalem candlesticks, surrounded by my wife and my children, savouring a wonderful meal, drinking sweet wine, contemplating my lot and feeling content and good and at peace. Do I *really* wish I were free to be doing the laundry or to be working on my taxes? Right ...

3. *Yom Hashoah* Lite

Sometimes pathetic behaviour can have rich spiritual worth, but other times it's just ... well, pathetic. I go back and forth on Purim, the Jewish holiday about which I feel the greatest ambivalence. It isn't that I don't *like* all the fun — the noisemakers and the masks and the drinking and the screaming children and all that — it's just that Purim has always seemed to me to be a great deal of effort about not too much at all. Not that I'm not glad old Haman didn't get his in the end — you may recall that Haman was the instigator behind an aborted pogrom in the old Persian town of Susa about twenty-five or so centuries ago whose plans were foiled by a combination of Queen Esther's bravery and her uncle Mordechai's cunning — because he certainly deserved the gallows for his efforts to destroy the Jewish people. I'm just not sure that one single pogrom backfiring on the villains who were planning it is really a good enough reason for the almost unbelievable kind of unbridled merriment that one finds in synagogues throughout the world on the evening of Purim.

And our synagogue is positively demure! I've been to synagogues where the liquor was flowing before, during and after the formal reading of the Scroll of Esther, the Biblical book that recounts the events Purim is supposed to commemorate. I've been to synagogues where the din was so deafening every time Haman's name was mentioned that it was almost painful. I was once even in a synagogue where the entire clerical staff — rabbi, assistant rabbi and cantor — came to the service in drag, dressed up like so many also-rans from

King Ahasueros' harem, the lovely (but not lovely enough) ladies Esther beat out in her efforts to save the Jewish people by marrying a Gentile king and becoming the queen of Persia.

Do I have to say in so many words what troubles me about all of this? That just barely fifty years after the ovens at Auschwitz finally cooled, the Jews are able to dance around in such giddy abandon over the downfall of a petty tyrant who didn't even manage to murder *anybody* before he and his ten sons ended up hanging from the gallows they had intended for Esther's uncle Mordechai and *his* family seems a bit forced to me. Perhaps a bit hollow as well. There is something that transcends mere silliness about Purim, something that approaches pathos in the truest sense of the word.

But, as I said above, pathetic behaviour doesn't have to be devoid of spiritual value. There is a certain satisfaction in damning the torpedoes and proceeding full-steam ahead into even the most pathetic situation, knowing perfectly well how the situation is going to seem to others and not much caring. Perhaps there is even a certain kind of nobility in continuing to observe Purim, in keeping the faith with an ancient hero despite the realities of more recent history. As I said, I approach Purim with ambivalence, not dislike. Or perhaps with a bit of dislike, but not with enough to consider, for example, *not* observing the holiday and *not* coming to synagogue (as though rabbis have the choice) to hear the Megillah read on Purim. (Megillah, which means "scroll" in Hebrew, is the colloquial name for the Biblical Book of Esther, which we indeed read in synagogue from a hand-written scroll. A lot of good it would do me not to come — I'm the one who reads the scroll to the congregation.)

So we do observe the holiday. We send the baskets of foods to our neighbours and give charity to the poor. We make a nice meal on Purim afternoon and eat our fill of *hamantaschen*, the traditional Purim pastries made of triangular slabs of glazed cookie dough filled with poppy seed paste or apricot preserves or the like.

We do it all and it always feels good in the doing. It's the contemplation of the absurdity of the whole enterprise that is the source of my ambivalence. I suppose that, in some larger sense, I do approve of Purim. I just can't quite reconcile those pleasant feelings with my sense of the Holocaust as a dark cloud looming over the festivities, a cloud of deeply pathetic absurdity that threatens, always, to rain on my parade.

Now, it's also true that the Jews have finally instituted a worldwide Holocaust Memorial Day. It comes just after Passover, about five or six weeks after Purim, and I suppose you can't make a totally fair comparison between a holiday that has been around for two and a half millennia and one that has only been formally observed for a couple of decades. But still, Holocaust Memorial Day—widely called in the Jewish community by its Hebrew name, Yom Hashoah — is a strange day, an oddly ritualless Jewish holiday when nobody knows quite what to do. We have resisted adding any passages to our prayers on Yom Hashoah — this, from a people whose prayers are sensitive enough to require liturgical adjustment several times in the course of the year to reflect seasonal variations in the climate in Israel — and, indeed, we have failed to institute any other rituals of even questionable profundity. It's almost as though the magnitude of the Holocaust were such that any attempt to capture the reality of the debacle in words would be absurd or, worse, pathetic.

Aside from lighting a memorial candle and saying my prayers with some extra melancholic fervour, I don't do much to mark Yom Hashoah. But that doesn't mean I don't esteem the *idea* behind the day. I *do* approve of having a day devoted to trying to focus on the magnitude and horror of the Holocaust, only, for me, that day is Purim. I have my requisite drink or two (although I never get quite drunk enough not to know the difference between Haman and Mordechai, as tradition would require) and I try to focus on the story of how our ancient foes were vanquished. But in my heart, I know what Purim means to me. There is a certain delight in Purim, a certain spiteful pleasure that derives precisely from *ignoring* the absurdity of the whole effort and celebrating the downfall of a tyrant who would have annihilated the Jewish people. Riotously.

There's something else. The Book of Esther is notable, among other things, for being the only book of the Bible in which the name of God is not mentioned. Now that's *not* to say that God plays no role in the story — the ancient rabbis vied with each other to identify the various spots in the story where divine intervention can be spotted and some ancient author even composed additions to Esther for the original Greek translation of the Bible that specified the role of the divine in the story. But it *is* to say that the role of God is subtle and easily missed in the tale, just like the presence of God in our modern lives. Perhaps that is why Purim continues to strike any chord at all in modern Jewish breasts — because the story describes people so much like us, people (unlike the heros of so many other Biblical stories) who have to *work* at identifying the role of God in their lives, people who could easily miss the point that there even *is* a role God plays in their lives.

It would be facile, even bizarre, to justify Purim by observing that, at least *eventually*, the Hamanites and the Hitlerites came to the same end. No, I think the only way to save Purim for post-Holocaust Judaism is to revel in the pathetic silliness of the festival, to find the strength to *enjoy* the holiday despite it all, to challenge God to inspire us *not* to be crippled by the inherent absurdity of Jewish history. The truth is that I like Purim more with each passing year. And I've stopped referring to it as Yom Hashoah Lite almost entirely, at least in public ...

4. Who We Are

I do a lot of speaking in non-Jewish settings — churches and schools and multicultural societies and venues like that. I usually give my standard "Judaism in Twenty-Three Minutes" speech and then take questions. And I always get the same questions, always the same requests to define Judaism in terms of other people's religions: why don't the Jews observe Christmas, why don't the Jews recognize Jesus as their messiah (usually phrased "Why did the Jews reject Jesus?"), why don't Jews feel the way Anglicans do about divorce or the way Catholics feel about abortion or the way Mormons feel about polygamy or the way the Muslims feel about the Quran or the way anybody in the entire world feels about anything at all that the questioner can think of.

They're all legitimate questions, I suppose, but there's also something annoying about them, something vaguely condescending and unmistakeably flip about questions that presume that the only way to define Judaism is to identify all the different ways the Jews have failed to adopt the tenets of other people's faiths.

I think I'll seize the bull by the horns next time and start off my remarks by telling my audience how Jews wish to see themselves. How Jewish history is more than an endless list of things other people did to us. How Judaism itself is more than simply the amalgam of what's left over when the Jews finally got finished rejecting everybody *else's* saviours, prophets and sages. I'll tell them how we wish them to see us. How we see ourselves.

First of all, I'll tell them that we are a community of faith. The point of Judaism isn't the obsessive perpetualization of Jewish rituals, but the establishment of a relationship of deep, ongoing spiritual communion between the God of Israel and each individual Jew. Not eating bagels or dancing the hora or planting trees in Israel, but knowing God and worshipping God and loving God. Not even following the dietary laws or keeping the Sabbath or lighting Hanukkah candles, but *using* those rituals as means to an end and not as superstitious gestures intended to make us *appear* pious in the eyes of others or to ward off some disaster we're convinced will immediately follow the ingestion of a piece of bacon. Not building synagogues or schools or Jewish community centres, but using the fellowship and knowledge those institutions can provide as a method of developing the *context* in which one can come, slowly, to believe in God and then, even more slowly, to know God and finally, as the crowning achievement of a Jewish life well lived, to love God with passion and fire.

Next, I'll tell them that we are a community of Scripture. Not fundamentalists and not know-nothing literalists, but simply a people of and by the Book, a people whose Torah lives in it as much as it lives inside of its Torah. The Book is not the point or the goal of worship and neither is its study the equivalent of worship. But, for us at least, text is context and the perimeters of Sacred Writ constitute the playing field on which we compete with our own baser instincts to win the prize that is faith in God and a life in God. I am quite aware (but thanks for pointing it out) that the Bible is filled with all the most ghastly stories of bigamy, treachery and slavery played out against an antique backdrop of animal sacrifice and ritual purity. I know all that and I see why it must seem like an unlikely vineyard for me to spend my spiritual life toiling in. But the book is a book about the relationship between a perfect God and an imperfect set of people and it has all sorts of fissures and warts and discrepancies in it. *It* is flawed in countless ways because it is the record of thousands of years of flawed people struggling to find some sort of avenue towards communion with God. And, for better or worse, it's *my* spiritual history in that book and I can't just put it down because some ideas in it don't suit some other ideas the world has developed in the meantime.

If anyone is still listening after all that, I'll tell them that we are a messianic community as well. If it's a Christian group I'm addressing that will get a rise out of them — the same people who spend so much time insisting that the Jews are almost by definition the people who *rejected* the messiah will, I expect, find it interesting to know that we haven't rejected the messiah at all. Or at least not the idea of a redeemer who will end history as we know it and usher in the age of peace of which the prophets spoke. The problem isn't really one of believing in the messiah, it's one of identifying him. So what's wrong with Jesus? Nothing, I guess. But he didn't actually manage to bring about any of the things the Bible says will come to pass in the wake of the messianic advent — no lions lying down with lambs, no dead rising from their graves, no knowledge of God sloshing up over the land like the waters cover the sea, none of that stuff — so, at least for the moment, we'll pass. Mind you, it's nothing personal. There have been dozens, maybe scores of people over the centuries who have proclaimed their messianic pretensions, not just Jesus of Nazareth. We give each the chance to back up (easy) words with (substantially harder) deeds and, at least so far, everybody has come up a bit short. So we keep waiting, but that doesn't mean we've given up on the basic idea or that we deserve to be crammed into ghettos or concentration camps as a result of our perceived intransigence. On the contrary, we're waiting precisely because we *haven't* given up, haven't relegated the *idea* of a personal redeemer to the steamer trunk in the attic of Jewish theology where our other antiquated, rejected dogmas get put. Anyway, as far as the messianic wait-it-out goes, we're in. Jews who say their prayers seriously pray for the arrival of the messiah three times every weekday and then again as many times as they say the Grace after Meals on any given day. It's a constant with us, a regular piece of the way we think about our destiny and about the destiny of the world. So don't swallow that nonsense about those loony Jews for Jesus being the "real" messianic Jews. All Jews are messianic Jews — for better or for worse, it's part of who we are and a big part at that.

So far, so good. Then, for my big finish, I'll end up by telling them that we Jews are the products of our own past. We *hate* it when people tell us that we are the people who rejected Jesus — as though all there were to Jewishness was the fact of not being some other -ness. The French aren't Albanians and the Mayans weren't Aztecs, but nobody seems to find that surprising or unreasonable. Only the Jews, it seems to me, get chastised over and over for *not* being somebody else. Well, take it or leave it, but we are who we are and not merely the people who aren't what you are. It's worse than just semantics, though — this idea, that the Jews are somehow doing something perverse by not adhering to somebody else's faith, is at the very core of the anti-Semite's uncanny ability to justify his own bigotry. Anyway, the point is that we are a people that exists by being who we are and not merely by not being who we aren't. Deal with it.

There are other things I could mention about the way Jews wish to be perceived by others, but I'd probably stop right there. If I make it to the front door without being attacked by people who are offended by *any* minority group asserting its right to self-definition, I'll consider my afternoon a success. Or maybe I should go back to taking questions about why Jews wear those little beanies when they pray ...

5. Nedarim Seyag Laprishut

If there's one part of Western culture that has always seemed the most alien and odd to me, it would have to be the glorification of asceticism. And it's not only a question of the celibacy of Catholic priests and nuns, either. The non-Jewish world seems to have accepted as part of its basic world view the idea that sensual pleasure is something to be squelched and limited wherever possible. They don't seem to enjoy eating much, for example. (Italians are an exception to this rule. Also the Greeks.) And they clearly don't feel comfortable making too much noise. And, say what you want, they do seem more than vaguely embarrassed about sex and they have indeed created a culture in which "dirty" means "sexy" and nobody, not even Supreme Court justices, seems able to tell the difference between pornography and eroticism.

Jews have never made very good ascetics. Our faith teaches us to think of sex as the sacred link between two mortals that can help them both attain the love of God. We usher in the Sabbath with wine and rich, yeasty breads. We eat well (and often) and we consider the feast that follows a wedding (or a bar- or bat-mitzvah or a circumcision) to be part of the religious ceremony — and an indispensable part at that. *Attending* a wedding is a privilege. But *dancing* at that same wedding before the bride and groom is a *mitzvah*, a method of worshipping God. True, we fast on Yom Kippur, but we make up for it by feasting the afternoon before the fast begins — and the ancient rabbis taught that the feast has the same piacular value as the fast. But most Jewish holidays are feast days, not fasts, and each is (rightly or wrongly) famous for its own gastronomic specialties. And on Purim, we drink.

Still, we're not talking black and white here. Everybody talks about people's sex drives, but the rabbis understood that there are also powerful drives within each of us prompting us to *fear* sensuality, to *avoid* indulgence in physical pleasure. There's a lot of ambivalence here in that we all *think* that we want nothing more than to embrace and enjoy the pleasures of the world. To prove just that point, we insist on seeking them out, even illicitly, convinced that we should be excused for our behaviour precisely because we are *driven* by irresistible forces, forces we describe glibly as *hormonal* or *genetically inherited* or even as *basic* to the human condition. But run as we all do towards pleasure, we also run away from it. We want it and we don't want it at the same time. We need it *and* fear it and we therefore both seek it *and* hide from it.

The Bible talks about somebody called a nazirite. This particular individual — Scripture specifically says that it can be a man or a woman — is described as somebody who wishes to renounce the world and who takes a vow to do so. The nazirite has to stay away from wine or liquor — even vinegar! — and remain in a state of utter purity. Male nazirites aren't even allowed the pleasure of shaving or having their hair cut.

The rabbis weren't impressed and one of them took a passage completely out of context to express his point. The Torah talks briefly about the case of a nazirite who becomes inadvertently defiled, specifying that it is thinking of the technical situation that would arise if somebody sitting next to a nazirite were to drop dead unexpectedly. Anyway, this rabbi — his name was Rabbi Eliezer Hakkappar — blithely ignores that detail and insists that the atonement ritual is meant to undo the sin of every nazirite, the sin inherent in having renounced pleasures God meant for the world. "For," the Talmud concludes, "it is the opinion of Rabbi Eliezer Hakappar that even an undefiled nazirite is called a sinner and that Scripture uses the word 'sin' with respect to a defiled nazirite because he has sinned twice (i.e. once by becoming defiled and once by becoming a nazirite in the first place.)"

Nedarim seyag laprishut, Rabbi Akiba says in the *Ethics of the Fathers* — vows are a fence around asceticism. The idea is clear and the implication sobering: better a little asceticism than a lot. If you feel overwhelmed by your inability to toe the line and to walk the straight and narrow, then by all means deny yourself something as a way of atoning for your weakness. Rabbi Meir reported that Adam himself had the right idea — after he realized that he was responsible for bringing death into the world, he set about atoning for his sins: he fasted for 130 years and gave up sex for 130 years and walked around in a scratchy, uncomfortable girdle fashioned of fig leaves for another 130 years. Rabbi Yochanan had a similar idea regarding King David — he atoned for his sin with Bathsheba by keeping ten especially beautiful concubines locked up in his palace in Jerusalem. He himself tended to them, braiding their hair and adorning them with jewels, but he wouldn't sleep with any of them as a way of atoning for his sin with another man's wife.

That kind of stuff is okay — *nedarim seyag laprishut!* — but only because it allows somebody to give up *something* without giving up *everything.* Accepting the pleasures of the world is a way of acknowledging its Creator, just like it's considered polite to open up a bottle of wine somebody brings over for dinner on the spot and serve it — you show your gratitude to your guests for their gift by using it, not by storing it away for a rainy day. The basic idea is that you are supposed to welcome God into your house, into your *space.* And He comes bearing gifts, gifts you are not supposed to accept with false gratitude and then hide away on the highest shelf in your linen closet with all the other junk people have brought you over the years.

So if we all worship the *idea* of pleasure and our Torah *commands* us to enjoy the pleasures of the world, what exactly is the problem? The problem, I guess, has to do with human nature, with the part of us that can't quite accept the fact that we are *worthy* of all these gifts. That's the paradox: we *aren't* all that worthy, yet we have still ended up somehow as the recipients of some of God's greatest gifts, gifts we know deep down (and also not that deep down) we don't really deserve. So we have a choice: enjoy them and feel guilty or renounce them and feel (miserable but) righteous. Judaism says: calm down and don't make such a big deal about everything. Do your best. Be a *mensch*. Worship the God Who made you by doing His commandments whenever you can and with as full a heart and as willing a spirit as you can muster. And accept the pleasures of the world as a way of acknowledging their (and your) Creator. I know plenty of people whose mental image of a true holy person would be a celibate, emaciated beggar wandering endlessly through the world in search of enlightenment. My personal picture of such a saint is a healthy man with a thirty-eight inch waist sitting at his Sabbath table surrounded by his wife and children, happy with his lot, grateful for his Torah, at peace with the God Who made him ...

6. In Which My Prayers Are Sometimes Answered

W hat could be more absurd than prayer? You stand still or sway gently back and forth with your eyes closed or fixed on the words in a book and you mumble inaudible words that you try to convince yourself are heard a billion trillion miles away by the God Who made the world, yea the whole universe, and Who rules it ... and Who also has nothing else scheduled for this afternoon except sitting on the Throne of Glory and listening to your whispered thoughts. Right. How about the guy next to you? Is God also listening carefully to what he's mumbling? How about the other million people who are saying their prayers exactly when you are — people in Malaysia and Finland and Zimbabwe and Ecuador? Is God listening to them too? All that assuming God really does speak all languages. And cares about all people. And is omnipotent enough to squelch the ineffable boredom He must experience when he hears the same words again and again and again and again and again and again, generally from the same people who want the same things they can't have or don't deserve or just won't get.

So if the theory is fraught with such problems, how about the actual practice? I mean, who cares about the prayers of everybody *else* in the world if you can prove that God actually does listen to *your* prayers? Most people's records are, I think, similar to mine. My mother had cancer for a decade and I prayed for her to recover. (She died.) I had a little tax problem a few years ago, so I bought a lottery ticket and prayed for the big one. (I lost.) You get the idea. On the other hand, some of the things I've prayed for over the years have indeed come to pass. A peaceful end to apartheid. Freedom of emigration for Soviet Jewry. A democrat in the White House. A sabbatical fellowship at Harvard. Sometimes these things take a bit of time — I got my puppy only this year, a full thirty years after I first thought to bypass my parents and bring the matter straight to the Creator of dogs — but it's undeniable: prayer works. Sometimes.

Now people seem strangely unwilling to accept prayer as an active agent in the affairs of the world. (No Nobels for me, even if I did pray for peace in South Africa.) And people seem equally unsure about how to relate to people like me who announce (in public, no less) that they play an immensely important role in the affairs of mankind because God, occasionally, answers their prayers. Actually, they aren't all that unsure at all — if you're a clergyperson, they humour you. And if you're not, they usually institutionalize you unless you can prove that you don't *really* mean that God takes His instructions from your whispered words of prayer and then acts on them. In other words, you're allowed to believe in prayer as long as you don't *really* believe in prayer. Otherwise, you're nuts.

The only thing stranger than the idea of prayer is the rationalization you hear from people who want to convince you that praying to God is a reasonable thing to do.

There are those who will tell you that God is all-powerful and is thus *entirely* capable of listening carefully to a billion people at the same time and responding on an individual basis, so denying the reasonableness of prayer is basically the same as denying the omnipotence of God.

Then there are those who tell you that God *always* does respond to the prayers of mankind, only that sometimes the answer is no. In other words, if you get what you pray for, that proves prayer works. And if you don't, that also proves prayer works, only that you didn't get what you were praying for. Great argument!

Then, there's my all-time favourite: prayer to God is a means of getting in touch with the spark of God inside us all. In other words, you rise in prayer before God not because you think God can hear you, but simply to get in touch with your own soul which — the thinking gets a bit fuzzy here — by virtue of having been fashioned by God in the first place is enough akin to its Maker to be able to ... to do something. I can't really finish the thought, because I've never been able to fathom what precisely it is your soul is supposed to do with your prayers once you've communicated them to it. Bear them to God when you sleep or when you die or something, I guess. If that sounds convincing to you, then I have a used prayerbook I'd like to sell ...

I suppose I should tell you now that I say my prayers every day. As often as I can, three times a day. Morning, afternoon and evening. Day in and day out, weekday and Sabbath, winter and summer, night and day. Prayer was the very first thing that drew me to Judaism as an adult, the single thing about life in the synagogue that seemed deeply enough attractive to make me consider changing my career plans in favour of a life in the rabbinate. When I first started attending synagogue services, it was the idea of prayer that drew me in, that made me feel that religion could be ennobling and deeply enough satisfying to warrant all the various sacrifices it demands in other arenas of our lives. And all that despite the inherent ridiculousness of the whole idea, the basically complete lack of empirical, verifiable evidence that prayer works, the obviously egocentric orientation of the concept behind the actual act and the grotesque problem of trying to believe that the same God who didn't hear the prayers of the million and a half Jewish children the Nazis slaughtered is going to be interested enough in you to listen while you pray for a promotion at work *if you really, really need the money.*

So why do I do it? I don't really know. I'm not crazy, I don't think. I don't talk to myself. I don't even talk to strangers if I can avoid it. I don't think I'm exceptionally egocentric, at least no more than is basic to the human condition. And I'm not especially given to talking to other invisible friends, not six-foot rabbits and not leprechauns and not ghosts. Well, ghosts, a little bit. But not fairies or elves or anything like that. I'm a rational man with an earned doctorate and no history at all of schizophrenia or other delusional conditions. And I pray. I say my prayers with whatever fervour I can muster, convinced that I am doing something noble and right and that my relationship with God is being thereby strengthened. I suppose in a certain sense, I say my prayers because, more than anything else, I am praying that there is a God who hears me. And yet that's too glib, too easy a way out. Because I don't *just* pray that there is a God, I also speak to my God and plead with Him and even bargain with Him a bit. The ancient rabbis used to say that it is worth doing a religious act even *not* for the right reasons, because by doing it at all you are at least leaving open the possibility of doing that same act one day for all the right reasons. Maybe that's how I've come to this inn, but it's not why I still live here. I believe in God and I believe — not rationally, not intentionally, not even really willingly — in the reality (if not the reasonableness) of prayer.

Should you pray too? Rabbis get paid to talk other people into saying their prayers, so I suppose I should say that you should. But *how* you should pray? It would be like teaching somebody how to make love or how to dance — the basic idea is teachable, but the actual process is something every individual has to dope out for himself. Good luck. I'll pray for you.

7. We Are What We Don't Eat

Whenever I host classes from one of the local senior high schools at the synagogue, the first question they ask almost always has to do with the dietary laws. Sometimes they know the word *kosher* and sometimes, most of the time, they don't. But they all know that Jews aren't supposed to eat bacon with their eggs and they always want to know why. (Members of my own congregation, by comparison, almost never ask me to explain the kosher laws to them — the ones with unkosher homes don't want to hear an explanation that will make them feel guilty and the ones with kosher homes are afraid they'll hear one that will make them feel foolish.) Anyway, I speak to high school groups quite often and when I ask for questions from the floor, the first one is usually why Jews hate pigs.

So after all these years, you'd think I'd have my answer straight. I do have an answer I usually offer, but just lately I've been asking myself if my answer is as totally honest as I wish it to be. Or, to put it a bit more charitably, I know two answers and I'm not as sure as I once thought I was which one is the right one.

Part of me thinks that the dietary laws are merely part of some Biblical effort at organizing the world. The Torah, after all, is fairly obsessed with the idea of honouring the Creator by showing respect for the intangible rubrics of creation. What that means in less fancy language is that the pious Israelite was expected to spend a lot of time drawing lines to separate things that are not supposed to be together. Maybe it's all practice for the *really* important task of dividing down the world into its godly and ungodly elements, the better to place oneself afterwards in the domain of the godly, or maybe the idea is *just* to show respect for the way the world was created by its Creator, but whatever — the Israelites spent a lot of time separating milk from meat, pure from impure, holy from profane, good from evil, Jewish from heathen, leavened from unleavened, tithed from untithed, workaday from sabbatical, licit from illicit and kosher from unkosher. They were very involved with the idea of establishing the precise boundaries of the Holy Land, but the Torah is equally concerned with the establishment of correct boundaries between neighbouring fields and between the different kinds of crops planted on any individual farmer's land.

In this context, the dietary laws are merely one more effort to divide the world down into godlike and godless domains. The kosher animals are the ones, then, that honour the ideals of the original plan — the mammals who chew their cud and have cloven hooves, for example, or the fish with fins and scales. The animals that don't fall squarely into one pre-conceived category or another — the camels who chew their cud but who *don't* have cloven hooves or the pigs whose hooves are okay but who don't chew their cud — somehow offend the whole system by merely existing. (Don't muddy the waters by insisting that God made the little piggies as well as the little lambs. Maybe it's a test.) Anyway, the animals that fall outside the original taxonomy are impure, unkosher, unfit for consumption — not tasteless or poisonous, only outside the sphere of zoological perfection. So people are given this task: to establish their fealty to the perfect God by ingesting only that which is perfect in His creation. The rest of the things you *could* conceivably eat — bats and camels and eels and turtles and snails — are for those who haven't figured out that the way to the Creator is via His creation.

But that's only what part of me thinks. Actually, I even think that this great exercise in dividing down the world into mutually exclusive, distinct domains probably *is* the correct framework for understanding the dietary laws as they appear in Scripture. But it isn't what makes them work for me personally and I don't think it's what makes them work for most people who observe them. I can't prove it — although I *might* have something to lean on in that the Biblical terminology, according to which animals, fish, insects and birds are either pure or impure, *has* been more or less totally dropped by Jewish people today in favour of the ubiquitous designation of food as being kosher or unkosher, words with no Biblical *cachet* or pedigree. (The word "kosher" only appears in the Bible one single time and it doesn't have anything to do with forbidden foods or dietary restrictions.)

The other reason I like the explanation I'm about to give you is that it also explains why so many Jewish people resist observing these laws with such perverse tenacity.

Judaism is a million paths to a single goal and that goal is the establishment of a relationship of deep, spiritual communion between each individual Jew and the God of Israel. Indeed, all of our rituals have as the common thread that binds them together the fact that they are all designed to inculcate some specific aspect of the faith in God we *wish* to develop in the people who undertake to perform them. So any nation can develop a myth about the creation of the world, but what is peculiarly Jewish about the creation story in the Torah is not its detail so much as its aftermath: we don't just tell the story, we live it (or better, we live inside of it), imitating its six plus one rhythm over the years and decades of a lifetime. And it works — after years of working six days and resting on the seventh, working six days and resting on the seventh, working six days and resting on the seventh, the idea that God made the world becomes part of us, part of who we are, part of how we see the world in which we live. It's a strange method, but it's very effective — and we Jews are not *only* keeping the Sabbath from week to week, but doing all the commandments as well. And, since each of them has a different aspect of the faith in God we wish to develop at its own generative core, we are constantly involved in the development of scores of *different* aspects of this faith in God we wish to have. It's sort of like living in a cocoon of faith that is constantly becoming more enveloping, more protective, more substantive and more substantial from day to day as we live our lives.

The cardinal thing about the dietary laws, I think, is their apparent arbitrariness. The Torah wants us to think of the world as God's home and of ourselves as guests in that home. Just as in our own day, that relationship, the one between guest and host, is governed by all the most specific rules of etiquette and good conduct — but the most important rule (*always!*) is that the guest show deference to the host by accepting his choices. Of menu. Of wine. Of company. Of table conversation. In other words, the guest in any culture shows subservience and gratitude to his host by *gratefully* accepting what is served for dinner without whining or moaning or sputtering about it — and certainly without asking if the hosts would mind cooking something *else* for dinner aside from what they had already chosen to serve. So it's the same way with the kosher laws — the Torah wants us to think of ourselves as guests in God's house and to behave like we mean it. The whole *point* of being a good guest lies in accepting (and then ignoring) the fact that the host's choices for the meal he is serving are completely arbitrary. The arbitrariness isn't at all a bad thing — the whole point of being a guest in the first place is that you trade in your prerogative to choose your own meal for the pleasure of having somebody else shop for it, pay for it, cook it, serve it to you and clean it up afterwards. Hosts and guests do not have a relationship of equality in any culture; indeed the whole idea of *being* a guest implies subservience and gracious good-naturedness about eating whatever slop your host thinks *he'd* like to eat for dinner on the night you're invited. You don't like it? Tough luck — and not only do you have to eat it, you have to insist you love it and (unless you really think you'll be sick) you have to ask for seconds after you've cleaned your plate. The whole point is that the guest is *supposed* to set his own feelings aside out of deference to the host; the relationship rests on the fact that the host calls the shots and the guest gratefully and graciously accepts the inequality of the situation as the price for a free meal.

So that's how I think the dietary laws are supposed to work, or at least how they do work for most of us. This world is God's house and we are all guests in it. Don't like what's for dinner? So make your own world and eat there. But as long as you're staying on in *this* world, you'll have to accept what its Host has chosen for dinner even if you *do* believe you'd like the pork chops more. Now there isn't anything *wrong* with pork chops — the whole point is that there's nothing wrong with any unkosher food — they're just not on the menu tonight. This isn't a police state we're talking about here; the whole point of behaving well as a guest rests in the fact that you don't have to. The idea is to rein yourself in *willingly* as a sign of gratitude to your hosts even if you *do* know more about menu planning than they do. (And no, this has nothing at all to do with the fact that the Bible so often likes to refer to God as the Lord of Hosts.)

I actually like observing the kosher laws. I suppose I do have *some* curiosity about foods our faith forbids to us. And I'm more than ready to accept that there's something weird about living in North America and *never* eating at MacDonald's or Burger King. But what can I say? I'm a guest at somebody else's table and I'm hoping to eat there for such a very long time that it's well worth the effort to try not to offend my Host ...

8. The Mask of God

Sometimes, I think of the Bible as a letter. A long, sometimes redundant letter, to be sure. But also a profound one — the kind you keep around in your desk drawer for years after you receive it and take out from time to time to read through again. Like all letters, this one often has more to do with the concerns of its writer than it has with the things that concern its readers, but it's not as bad as all that either — the letter may have been written by somebody else, but it has come into my possession and so, at least after the fact, I'm a part of it too. But there are also problems with this letter. For one thing, the letter is unsigned, so I don't really know who wrote it. For another, I didn't get the letter from the postman in the normal way; I sort of found it myself as a result of some surreptitious rummaging in my grandparents' attic, so I can't be sure I'm even *supposed* to be reading it. On top of all that, the envelope is long gone, so there's no way to know who the original addressee was or how he would feel about my reading his mail.

Other times, I think of the Bible as a jigsaw puzzle, a vast, cosmic puzzle meant for the edification and spiritualization of mankind. But the puzzle pieces are scattered, some in the book itself, others in ruins spread across the ancient world. Still other pieces are hidden in the lost books of obscure ancient authors, where they await discovery by clever, patient scholars. Some pieces are even hidden within the human breast, where they live in lofty (if unacknowledged) seclusion until people learn how to look deeply enough within themselves to find them. The goal of Bible study, then, is the piecing together of this vast puzzle on the assumption that the puzzle will yield a message of the grandest importance once it is correctly solved. But there's a problem here as well: since no one has ever seen the completed puzzle, no one can be certain what the message is or why it is so urgently worth deciphering.

Still other times, I find myself thinking of the Bible as a mirror. There's an old parable I like to repeat that sets this image out pretty clearly. It's about a man who is seated in his barber's chair with his back to the front door while he has his hair cut. When the barber is through cutting his hair, he holds up a hand mirror so that the man can see his barber's work. At that very moment, however, the king passes by in front of the shop. The barber hears the commotion and looks out the door directly at the king.

Struck by the majesty of his king and by his uncanny good fortune to have looked up at precisely the right moment, he calls to his client, "Turn around and look out the door, the king is about to pass out of view!"

"No need," the client responds coolly, "I can see him in your mirror."

The barber in this parable is a prophet, perhaps even Moses himself who saw God face to face, and his customer represents the rest of us. The customer doesn't turn his head to see the king, because he cannot and may not — aside from the fact that no one may gaze on God and live, he would have been too late anyway — and he therefore has no option but to rely on the blurred image of God he can perceive in his barber's mirror. The mirror, of course, is the Bible and it's a good symbol. The mirror is not that complicated a machine. It's hardly a machine at all, only a piece of polished metal that the prophets and saints of old hold up to our eyes that we may see at least the outline of the king as he passes by. The narrative tells us all sorts of things about God, about our chances for communion with Him, about our potential for intimacy and union with the God of Israel. But it is all misshapen and fuzzy, all filtered through the looking-glass of human language and experience. It is, by definition, the indescribable described, the ineffable pronounced, the limitless fenced in by the puny limits of language and human speech and the only slightly less pathetic boundaries of poetry and song. God exists, but He presents Himself obscured behind the veil of human expression, imprisoned within the confines of the ability of His creatures to fathom Him, a hazy image in a barber's mirror, an echo still reverberating in the night after the animal that made the sound in the first place has lumbered off to its lair and gone to sleep.

And then, on still other occasions, I find myself thinking of the Bible as a mask, as the mask of God, as the mask God wears when He approaches individuals unable for one reason or another to gaze upon His face. We study the mask, but that's only because it's there. What we really would like is to see behind the mask, to see who's wearing it and what the mask-wearer would look like *without* the mask. But there's no way to do it, at least no way for average people. All we can do is try to peer through the eye-holes, but even that is not very satisfactory. In fact, you can't really see anything, only that there *is* somebody there, that the mask isn't being worn by a doll or a mannikin or a ghost.

And then, after years of looking at the mask and trying to peep through the eye-holes, it strikes you that, for better or worse, the mask is all you're ever going to see. Its contours, its lines, its expression ... they are either intimately or remotely connected to the face behind it, but you can't tell. You wish you could know more, but, eventually, you accept that you can't know, that you won't ever know. At first you're angry with the mask for obscuring that which lies beyond it. Then, slowly, as maturity comes, you realize that the mask itself is precious. You see it with new eyes, with new respect. It no longer seems forbidding, but almost enchanting. You forget your irritation with its nature and concentrate on enjoying it for what it is ...

9. The Long and Short of Jewish Life

The festivals of the Jewish year are a strange collection of days. Some, like Chanukah, have been elevated to positions of prominence completely out of proportion with their real importance in the traditional scheme of Jewish things, while others have lapsed into desuetude despite impeccable Biblical and post-Biblical credentials. Still others had already fallen into such obscurity in *ancient* times that even the rabbis themselves despaired of finding too much deep meaning in them. And then there's the bizarre, more than slightly masochistic custom of doubling most of the holidays from one to two days in Jewish communities outside of Israel.

The rationale for observing two days of most festivals — that it was impossible for diaspora Jews to know when the new month had been proclaimed in Jerusalem — was *already* passé in late antiquity once the calendar was fixed and published and the Talmud's own justification for keeping on with the two-day format — that they had no right to depart from the custom of earlier generations — is as forced as it is spurious. But what does any of that matter? No one observes these "second" days anymore for any discernable rational reason anyway — and you can be sure that we have managed to find the fortitude to depart from any number of other customs of our ancestors when we felt compelled to do so for one reason or another. Instead, they're mostly observed because they serve so nicely as a way of making a statement to the rest of the Jewish world about the level of one's own piety. And how can things like logic or ancient calendars be expected to compete with motivation like that?

Anyway, the Jews have such a fixation on the whole concept of length that almost every authentic Jewish ritual is too long by at least a third. The Grace After Meals, for example, is oddly, almost absurdly long — eight or nine pages in most prayerbooks — when compared with the brief three-benediction formula even the ancient rabbis admitted was all Scripture itself requires. (There were also other versions in ancient times, one of which was no longer than five words.) The synagogue service on Saturday mornings itself is also ridiculously long in most synagogues. Developed around a core of prayer that lasts, maximum, fifteen minutes, there are synagogues today that expect their worshippers to sit still for three or four *hours* instead. The old custom of the Palestinian Jews of reading the Torah over a three-year period was widely scrapped in favour of the single-year cycle of the Babylonian Jews — thereby tripling the amount of time it takes to read the weekly lesson — and has only been re-introduced recently in synagogues anxious to shorten their service in a strictly traditional way. The famous Passover *seder* meal falls prey to the same obsessive need to lengthen what was originally brief, to the point and elegant in its focus *and* brevity — and then, after you finally *do* conclude the festive meal and you have managed to wade through all the added verbiage designed (one can only assume) to bury the simple meaning of the festival under a mountain of obscure poetry and imported liturgy, you get to clean it all up and go to bed so you can get up the next day and start preparing to do the whole thing over a second time on the next night.

The notion that length is a desirable quality in liturgy is a bizarre one at best. Most of us can hardly focus on *television* shows that last too long, let alone muster up the kind of intense concentration that is theoretically the *sine qua non* of legitimate prayer. Pulling it all together to stand in prayer before God requires a lot: letting go of the peripheral and tangential, focusing intensely on the task at hand, finding the internal courage to repress the sense of almost crippling absurdity any thinking individual must bring to the whole *concept* of prayer in the post-modern age, and, of course, locating enough meditative strength to recite the words of one's prayer with meaning and fortitude. How long can anyone do all of that? I'll tell you from my own experience: a few minutes. Maximum. After that, my mind wanders. My concentration wanes. My doubts rise and interfere with my ability to say my prayers with the pristine intensity I feel should be the *least* one brings to personal prayer. My feet start to hurt.

Still, religion is at least three-fifths show biz these days — and you can't expect to get people to give up their Saturday morning golf to come to synagogue if you're not going to give them their money's worth. So we continue to lengthen the service, adding more and more verbiage and unnecessary blather to what was originally a compact, attractive liturgy. We have come to esteem especially those cantors who can lengthen the service the most by dragging their prayers out with endless melisma and operatic flourish. Rabbis aren't immune either — the longer one's sermons, the more intelligent one is generally presumed to be. (It doesn't seem to matter that this is obviously not the case and that, if anything, just the opposite is probably true. What matters here is one's ability to *impress* people by talking for a very long time.)

It seems to me that all the most important spiritual acts can be accomplished in an instant: repentance, supplication, confession, worship, acknowledgement, commitment, engagement and prayer. The true prayer is the one that is over *before* it can be uttered, that exists in the inexpressible context of the worshipper's ongoing relationship with God far more really than it ever can once forced into the manacles of human language. Prayer is an elusive thing, as is worship. But as anyone who has ever been in an unhappy relationship will easily confirm, lengthening false declarations of love doesn't transform them into the real thing, it only makes them long and doubly painful to those who have to sit through them.

10. Sex

I don't think there's any area in which we Jews have shot ourselves more devastatingly in the foot by aping the Gentile world to our own detriment than in the area of human sexuality. Why the West has done to sex what it has, I can't say, although I have my theories. And who's to blame, I also can't say, although I have my theories about that too. But whoever is ultimately responsible for teaching an entire world to think of human sexuality as something inherently dirty and sinful has not done the world a favour. On the contrary: an awful disservice — and the worst part is that it didn't have to be that way.

One of the most basic tenets of Judaism is that everything that exists in this world God created exists for a reason and can be used either poorly or well. This isn't quite what the Buddhists teach about all things having elements of yin and yang in them — Judaism teaches that inanimate and intangible things have no moral or ethical status at all inherent in them. It is people who have the moral imperative to use the things God made in the world either wisely or to their own detriment. So fire can either burn in the Sabbath lamps as a spur to the worship of God or it can be the arsonist's tool of destruction. Wine can either be the downfall of the alcoholic or an agent of ritual sanctification of the highest degree. Even a knife can kill in a murderer's hands or else be used to slaughter the goose for a wedding feast.

Sexuality is in the same category as are all the rest of the intangible things that await us in this world. Certainly, the rabbis teach, the point of creating human sexuality was not to populate the world — could not the same God who made Adam and Eve have created as many billion people as He wanted if that had been His wish? True, the very first of the Torah's commandments is to go forth and multiply, but I'm asking a different question here, not *whether* we are commanded to procreate, but *why* God chose such an odd, complicated, almost uncontrollable method to populate the planet. After all, He did fill the oceans with fish all at once. As the book says, "Let the waters bring forth swarms of living creatures!"

No, the point of sexual desire is not anywhere near so much to make babies as it is to suggest to small-minded human beings what love and passion are supposed to be about. And since God Himself wishes not merely to be loved, but to be loved passionately, does it not follow that He had some sort of self-imposed obligation to provide a model that ordinary mortals could understand of the kind of selfless, passionate love that He hopes to inspire in His creatures with respect to His awful (that is, awe-full) Self? The Bible commands the love of God, but which of us would otherwise be smart enough to know what that could possibly mean without a little divine guidance? So we are provided with a series of models, each one contributing to our sense of precisely how we might go about fulfilling that commandment. First we have parents on whom we depend and for whom we feel deep filial affection. Then we grow a bit older and have our first friends, other children who teach us how to care about people who care about us and how to give to others and all the other lessons we learn from our childhood friends. Then, in adolescence, we form even tighter friendships and find out even more explicitly what it means to feel bound up with other people and to know others intensely, even intimately.

And then, somewhere along the way, we discover love. We fall in love with another and learn that true love can be passionate, physical, reciprocal and deep all at the same time. That mature love is humbling without being humiliating, selfless without being selfish, physical and deeply sensual without being obscene, lewd or smutty. And that honest love is so attractive to us, so deeply correspondent to something deep within, that we know at the very moment we first experience it that we will never rest until we make that kind of love a permanent feature of our lives.

This kind of love — sensual, sexual, overwhelmingly passionate and deeply, utterly consuming — is not a mere happenstance of creation, but a gift, perhaps the greatest gift, of God to mankind because it is from that kind of love that springs the potential to love God Himself. The desire for physical love between human beings is merely (merely!) supposed to be the spur to loving God no less passionately than any individual lover loves his or her lover here on earth. Human sexuality is the key to the love of God no less certainly so than the horror of death is the key to fearing Him. And that, in a nutshell, is why sex is neither dirty nor indecent nor inherently pornographic: because it has the potential to inspire the love of God.

So much for theory. But the truth is that we live in a misshapen, deformed world in which even the greatest of God's gifts is misperceived as a detriment to religious accomplishment rather than taken as an impetus to attain ever greater heights of spirituality.

We Jews celebrate children's coming of age — the famous bar- and bat-mitzvah — at puberty precisely *because* we assume that the performance of the commandments (most of which much younger children could easily be taught to perform) can have no meaning outside of the worship of God — and that the worship of God can not be truly accomplished by somebody not even yet on the spectrum of sexual passion. True, thirteen-year-olds are hardly sexual veterans with adult abilities to understand the meaning of love and passion. But, by virtue if of nothing else than at least of *being* pubescent, they are finally *somewhere* on the spectrum of human sensuality and therefore have the nascent *potential* — real, if inchoate — to understand what it can possibly mean for the Torah to command us to love God.

Because that is the point, the only point, of all our observance. The point of keeping a kosher home is not keeping a kosher home anymore than the strict observance of the Sabbath laws has the observance of the Sabbath as its point. The point of both — and of all the other rituals and commandments of traditional Judaism — is the worship of God and that, we have come to understand, can only be accomplished by somebody who understands what love is.

This, incidentally, is why the debate currently raging in the world about homosexuality and the place of homosexuals in society is (or ought to be) a bit of a Jewish red herring. The point is that sexuality and sensual love are gifts from God to us all, gifts designed to inspire us to love God with the same passion we experience on earth. That there are two short passages in Scripture proscribing one specific act that male homosexuals might otherwise perform with each other hardly seems too important a point in the larger scheme of things — and is at any rate balanced, actually outweighed, by a far longer list of sexual deeds forbidden to heterosexuals. The Bible prohibits certain sexual acts for the same reason, I suppose, that it forbids us to eat certain foods — not because eating this or that kind of meat is somehow wrong or bad, but merely to remind us where the food comes from and who, precisely, the Author of sustenance is. The sexual prohibitions — and there are not really very many of them — have the same point: to remind us who exactly created love and created us and who it is who loves us and who wishes us to spend our lives seeking His love. That different sexual acts will appeal to different people is not any more amazing than the fact that different people like different foods: if you like lamb chops, you win; if you like pork chops, you lose. But the point is that the same kosher laws apply to all Jewish people *regardless* of whether they like one or the other and the same applies to the sexual prohibitions as well. To determine an individual's worth and worthiness based on the nature of his or her nutritional appetites *or* sexual predilections seems to me to be missing the point entirely when the totality of all Jewish spiritual endeavour has as its common and only goal the passionate, all-consuming love of God. Why should anyone have a problem with that?

11. Snatching Failure from the Jaws of Defeat

The challenge of any successful religious civilization is not to avoid failure, but to learn to deal with it. And indeed, the history of the religions of the world is littered with the corpses of defunct faiths that couldn't do it, religions that were so shackled by their own dogmatic beliefs that they simply couldn't adapt when the moment of decision came. Judaism has survived systemic failures so often that you might say we are a religion that has elevated failure to the level of profound spiritual success. This has been a pattern for so long that we hardly notice it anymore. But we are faced, in our very own day, with a failure of traditional dogma so all-encompassing and so potentially destructive that I think we ignore this particular aspect of our history at our own peril. Having made such a remarkable statement, I suppose I have to explain it.

Let's start back with the Bible. If you arrived from Mars and simply began to read the Hebrew Bible without any prior knowledge or preparation, you would imagine that the society being described in its pages could not possibly exist outside of its own land. The whole religious system described in the pages of Scripture has as its absolutely most basic assumption the fact that Israel is a nation whose religious life is inextricably bound to its land. Sin is expiated through a complicated system of animal sacrifice centred in the Temple in Jerusalem. Indeed, sacrifice outside the Temple is not merely discouraged, but forbidden in the most deliberate, unambiguous language possible. The observance of the Sabbath and of the festivals, the laws governing the various relationships between individuals, even the worship of God itself — these are all tied to Jerusalem and to the Temple, to the land and to the gratitude its inhabitants are expected to feel towards the God Who took His people from slavery in Egypt and brought them triumphantly (if only eventually) into the land He promised would be theirs for all eternity.

Then, debacle. The ten northern tribes were exiled to the east by the Assyrians in the eighth century B.C.E. and never heard from again. The southern tribes were all that was left and then they were exiled from *their* land in the beginning of the sixth century. The whole system ended — no more sacrifices, no more festivals, no more worship, no more tithes, no more anything that the Torah holds up as absolutely essential for the spiritual, even the physical, preservation of the nation. But the exiles didn't disappear, didn't simply vanish into the Babylonian countryside to re-emerge as new, non-specific citizens of the Babylonian melting pot. Instead, their leaders switched gears and developed a theology of exile that allowed the people to see their catastrophe as an (at least theoretically) positive experience. The point of exile was to cleanse and purify, they taught, to create an experience of dependence on God that would rival, even possibly surpass, the experience the ancestors of the exiles had as they wandered through the desert on their way to the Promised Land and were dependent on God for the water they drank and for the manna they ate and for the clothing they wore. The theology simply adapted and, as a result, the people survived.

But that was hardly the biggest failure of doctrinal theology in Jewish history. And besides, to the extent that the exile could be described as a fitting punishment for a rebellious people, it wasn't necessarily a crisis of such awful theological proportions at all.

From its earliest religious stirrings, Israel was a monotheistic nation. The belief in one God is so basic as to be presented in Scripture as an optionless feature of Israelite thought as early as the first of the nation's ancestors. But to establish a relationship with that one God, especially once the theologians of ancient Israel determined that His regular residence was in the sky, high above the world He created for humanity to inhabit, was another problem. The twin institutions of the priesthood and the prophetic caste were developed to speak directly to that most basic of all religious requirements: the need to be able to communicate with God and to experience communication from God on an individual, ongoing basis. It worked like this: the priests conveyed the wishes and prayers of the people to God by serving in His temple and offering up the offerings and sacrifices that were the physical embodiments of the people's spiritual longing for communion with God. And the prophets spoke in the name of God to the people, bringing specific messages from the divine realm to earth and allowing the people to feel the dynamic presence of a communicative, if never quite loquacious, God in their midst.

The system worked well. The prophets proclaimed the word of God and the priests carried the offerings of Israel back to God and the dialogic path was cleared and ready for the spiritual wanderer to tread. And then, failure. Unprecedented, unexpected failure of the entire system. The prophets disappeared. Just stopped being around. Where did they go? Why were there prophets up until a certain moment and then no more? Why did the institution simply wither and die? I suppose the obvious answer would be that God simply finished saying what He had to say and therefore didn't need any more spokespeople. Years later, the rabbis insisted it was all a function of Israel's own unworthiness, but that sounds more like after-the-fact rationalization than anything else. And then, the other shoe dropped: the Temple was destroyed in the first century C.E. by the Romans and never rebuilt. The priesthood carried on briefly, then stopped functioning almost entirely.

The faith founded on the priest and prophet ought to have died out, ought to have become as defunct as its most basic institutions had now become. But again, Judaism managed to survive. The rabbis learned to hear the word of God booming forth from between the lines of Scripture, so that the Torah became the latter-day prophet that spoke the word of God directly and specifically to the people. The synagogue came, at least eventually, to take the place of the Temple, providing a place and space for people to speak their aspirations, prayers and hopes directly to the God who used to be approachable only through the sacred portals of the Jerusalem sanctuary.

But there were further failures as well. The whole rabbinic movement ran out of steam and petered out at a certain moment in history, the bold willingness of the rabbis of the mishnaic and talmudic periods to study Scripture and mine in its quarries for new interpretations and new takes on old rituals suddenly stunted by a massive failure of nerve sometime around the sixth century of this era — a failure which has led to generations of devout pupils whose connection to those ancient quarries consisted and continues to consist merely of contemplating the ore hewn by others. Still, derivative and diminished though it may be, we have constructed a religious civilization based precisely on the study of the works of the ancient rabbis, convincing ourselves (against all logic) that we are somehow communing with the words of Torah by refusing to accept as valid any interpretations not thought of by other people in other times and codified in *their* books. It's a bit silly and more than a bit pathetic, but it's worked so far. Again, success from failure, honey from the lion's carcass.

And now: the Holocaust. I've already written about the impossibility of speaking in traditional theological categories after the Shoah, so I'll content myself with saying that the jumping-off point of any cogent post-Holocaust theology has to be that the deal, the much vaunted covenant between God and Israel, is off. After all, what rabbi can seriously tell his people to honour the covenant by not eating pork rinds or by not smoking on Saturdays when God Himself seems to feel free to drop the ball whenever He wishes even if a million and a half children die as a result? It wouldn't be too much to say that all of traditional Jewish theology rests on the foundation stone of the covenant between God and Israel, but the system of belief and practice based on that covenant has failed on such a massive scale that it seems almost impossible to imagine restoring it with mere words. For the most part, rabbis simply ignore the whole issue, preferring to mutter about divine justice when they are absolutely required to say something. Does anybody believe it? Is there really somebody in the world who thinks that millions were shot into execution pits and asphyxiated in gas chambers because God was irritated with the Jewish people's apparently endemic laxness in Sabbath observance? Are there really people who can insist that the systematic destruction of not hundreds, but thousands of entire Jewish communities need not be seen as a rupture of the basic covenant that is supposed to bind the Jewish people and the God of Israel?

New terms need to be developed, new ideas worked out. A new *concept* of the covenant needs to be established if Judaism is going to keep from degenerating in the wake of the Holocaust into a system of superstition and silliness. We've rescued ourselves before when the system has gone down irretrievably and utterly. Can we do it again? Can we resuscitate Judaism before the coma becomes irreversible? Can we survive?

12. Packing Them In

No synagogue is big enough on the High Holidays, the great fall festivals of Rosh Hashanah and Yom Kippur which are, respectively, the Jewish New Year and the Day of Atonement. In fact, the sanctuaries of most synagogues these days are being built with removable walls at the back so that the same rooms which easily accommodate the congregation for the other 362 days of the year can be expanded to twice, sometimes to three times their normal size for the High Holidays.

It's a phenomenon. And it's one that shows no signs of letting up. On the contrary, my synagogue gets more and more requests for seats each year, often from complete strangers or from people whose only connection to Judaism is this inexplicable annual need to spend a few hours in the bosom of a traditional Jewish community at prayer.

I suppose it's the same for other religions. I know that churches often have amazing attendance at Christmas, for example, and I suppose that a great many of those worshippers too must be people who have no particular use for organized religion during the rest of the year. But there's a big difference too: Christmas is supposed to be fun. Turkeys and hams. Santa and Rudolf. Enough presents to keep retailers warm until it really is warm outside. Stockings and eggnog and wassail (whatever that is) and Christmas trees and all that stuff. Non-Christians, of course, hate having all that fun crammed down their throats whenever they dare enter a public place in December, but for people on the inside, what could be more fun than Christmas?

Rosh Hashanah is significantly less fun than Christmas. And Yom Kippur is even less fun than Rosh Hashanah. Together, they frame a dour ten-day week of merciless self-analysis and introspection, of regretful coming to terms with a litany of personal weaknesses, inadequacies, failures and shortcomings. We are bidden during the High Holiday season to focus the spotlight on the innermost chambers of the human heart and, worse, to face the consequences of such searching interior investigation. It is a season of repentance and hope for the future, to be sure. But that hope is, at least ideally, to be founded on a kind of self-knowledge and self-awareness that even the *most* pious have to find upsetting and a bit unnerving.

We start out hopefully on Rosh Hashanah with family get-togethers and long, if basically upbeat prayers. We harp on the fact that Rosh Hashanah is meant to be the birthday of the world, the anniversary of creation. We describe ourselves as putty in the hands of God (thereby downloading some of the guilt for our shortcomings on the Fashioner of our weak wills and inadequate characters) and as happy, dumb sheep who pass beneath the shepherd's staff one by one as he counts them and assesses them with love and devotion. (It is, after all, the *shepherd's* fault, not the sheep's, if a wolf gets to the flock.) We eat apples dipped in honey as a hopeful sign of a sweet new year and we fling bread crumbs into nearby streams of rushing water in the somewhat mysterious hope that the crumbs will take our sins along downstream to the ocean where, presumably, the crumbs *and* the sins will get dissolved (or at least lost) in all that water.

Then, on Yom Kippur, the mood is different. A sense that the jig is up permeates the sanctuary. The services are long — in our synagogue, we go two hours on Kol Nidre evening, five hours for the morning services the next day and then another two or three hours in the afternoon. We fast. We don't drink. The punctiliously observant don't wear leather shoes as a way of increasing their discomfort during the long portions of the service which are recited standing. No sex. No bathing, at least not for pleasure. No perfumes for the women or after-shave for the men. No shaving at all, for that matter. None of the things most people consider vital for their comfort and sustenance. A day of serious prayer devoted to the contemplation of the most serious defects in our lives, our personalities and our selves. We consider the various ways we have ruined (or at least weakened) our relationships with our parents and our children, with our spouses and siblings and friends. We beat our breasts and recite litany after litany of sin, damning ourselves over and over as the authors of our own misfortune.

By the end of the day, I'm always very tired. My eyes hurt. My feet hurt. My breath is sour. I'm hungry. My voice is practically gone. I feel greasy and itchy. The fun I recall having had only ten days earlier flinging my sins like dust into the stream seems forced and absurd. I regret my stubbornness and my sloth, my many inadequacies and weaknesses. I feel failed as a father and as a son, as a husband and as a friend. I have the vague sense that I will try to do better in the future, but my resolve is weakened by the awful knowledge that I feel this way every year and yet seem incapable of effecting any real change in my life no matter how deeply sincere my plans are after fasting on my feet for twenty-five hours. Christmas, it's not.

And yet, they come. In droves. We actually issue tickets for specific seats in the sanctuary on the High Holidays because there are so many people competing for them and our congregation needs to guarantee that the members who pay the bills don't get shut out of their own synagogue because they arrive too late in the morning. Why do you think they come? Do people *like* feeling awful? Do people feel good about feeling bad? Is there something noble, even perversely pleasurable, about owning up to one's shortcomings in public and before God Himself like an adult? Yes to all the above, but that's not quite all. There's something else, something harder to describe that draws the people in, something that makes the day attractive to people in the most literal sense of the word.

I think that the secret of the phenomenal success of the High Holidays lies in the fact that they collectively constitute the Jewish season of being taken seriously. Most people feel marginalized in most areas of their lives. They work for business that could exist easily without them. They pay taxes to municipalities that would be able to pick up the trash even without their tax dollars. They have never voted in an election on any level of government that would have had a different outcome if they themselves had cast their vote differently. The most respect they get from anybody comes from retailers anxious to sell them something — and the more expensive the item involved, the more fawning attention they get (and the less they like it). In every measurable way we can consider the lives we lead, we don't count. And our actions don't count. And we ourselves don't count for much either — and if you bristle at that thought, just ask yourself precisely what impact *your* death is going to have one day on the world. Sorry to have brought it to your attention.

And so they come, one Jew at a time, through the doors of our sanctuary on the High Holidays. Not to party or to make merry, not to dance or to laugh, but to count for something. To be taken seriously. To believe, even for a few hours, that their deeds are profoundly important. That their actions have consequence. That their shortcomings damage the world. That their sins are rips and tears in the fabric of being. That they matter more than they thought, not only in the eyes of God, but in their own eyes as well ...

13. One Nation Under God

Unity, specifically Jewish unity, is Jewish apple pie: the one concept that enjoys universal lip support from all quarters at all times. No one can oppose it, no one who hopes for recognition as a Jewish leader would dare do anything that would suggest even obliquely that preserving the unity of the Jewish people is not his or her paramount concern. I have something I'd like to say about the unity of the Jewish people, but I'll have to preface my remarks by telling you something about the private zodiac.

I've written in several places about my idea that the basic premise of astrology — that there are particular stars and combinations of stars that affect, influence and even control our destinies — is true only in that we all have personal zodiacs of individuals and configurations of individuals that rotate and orbit around us exerting different levels of influence and gravitational force on us at different moments in our lives and affecting us in ways which only *seem* magical and beyond human comprehension. Thus is it possible for my fictitious Roman scientist, Nigidius Figulus, to teach that it is possible "for an individual of undistinguished lineage and limited education to be thrust into greatness, not because of any personal merit, but merely by virtue of existing at the confluence of metaphysical vectors unknown to, and unsensed by, the individual in question".

Nigidius Figulus may well be right, but, for most of us, the challenge inherent in the private zodiac is primarily to identify the various constellations that lie along its path. At first, this may seem like a simple task as we assign spots to parents, grandparents, teachers, siblings, friends, spouses, Little League coaches, spiritual leaders, choir leaders and scout leaders who have influenced us and who continue to influence us one way or the other. But the situation is rendered dramatically more complicated once we realize that there is more to the universe than can be seen by the naked eye.

Unaided, we can see some of the planets and the occasional asteroid, but the earth is constantly being affected by the gravitational pulls of distant stars that are completely invisible to the naked eye. Even with all but the most powerful telescopes, countless heavenly bodies remain invisible to us even though scientists can easily identify the ways in which they pull and tug at us. Still other heavenly bodies remain unknown and unidentified even though they seem as though they ought to exist, their theoretical presences merely *sensed* by our scientific instruments here on earth without anyone knowing *exactly* where they may be found.

The same set of phenomena applies as well to the private zodiac, which may thus be populated by many invisible personalities, personalities we can only perceive through the introspectional equivalent of the radio telescope *if* we know where in the dark sky to look in the first place. And, just as we see by the light of dead stars every night of our lives, any number of the personalities and individuals who orbit on our private zodiacs may well be long gone. The light of dead stars is a famous phenomenon: a star explodes and disappears from the universe, but its enormous distance from earth guarantees that we terrestrials continue to see the star as it existed millennia ago before it became first a supernova and then, eventually, a thin cloud of cool interstellar dust. That we live out our lives under the direct influence of any number of dead stars that only *appear* to exist along our own private zodiacs is less empirically provable, although it is becoming more and more obvious to me with every passing year of my own life.

I have come to believe in ghosts. Not in the spooks and spectres of Hollywood movies, but in the phantasmic projections of the long dead who appear to me to live on even now because I can only perceive them as they were when their image was sent out to me, not as they are today. My own private zodiac is populated more by ghosts

than by the living, but there's nothing much to be done about it —
I'm not sure how one goes about changing the constellations along
one's private zodiac. I'm not even sure we *can* change them. It's quite
enough to identify them properly in the first place. But to do that,
we have to understand ourselves well enough to know where to look.

Now what is true of individuals is also true of nations. The Jewish people, for example, has its own private zodiac, its own personal
circuit of constellations that hover and twist in endless orbit around
the collective heads of the people. But the individuals and constellations of individuals that constitute the private zodiac of the Jewish
people all have their *own* private zodiacs rotating in timeless orbit
around *them*, as do those individuals and *their* zodiacal signs and so
on and so forth. The common destiny of the Jewish people is not,
therefore, merely a philosophical conclusion we draw by considering
the common Jewish past and projecting it into the future. Or rather,
it *is* that, but it's also a part of the physical nature of the Jewish
people that endures as the interlocking and interlinking orbits and
circuits of countless private zodiacs pass by each other in an endless
progression of orbits within an ever shrinking and expanding set of
infinitely concentric circles. Jewish individuals are linked to each
other by blood, to be sure. And those same Jewish people are linked
to each other emotionally by having experienced a common past.
But the common future of the Jewish people is guaranteed by the
gracefully interlaced orbits of an endless succession of private constellations whizzing by in impossibly un-unravelable chains of pitch
and yaw, each one effecting its own individual influence not on one
or two other planets in the Jewish universe, but upon hundreds and
thousands of others, some intensely close and others remarkably distant. As the stars chase after each other and tug at each other's
gravitational fields with internal strength all the more mysterious for
being both undeniable and ineluctable, a common destiny is woven,
a destiny fashioned of divinely interspliced helices of national aspira-
tion and divinely ordained fate.

The unity of the Jewish people is, therefore, not merely a politi-
cally desirable condition to be sought as a means of defense against
the kind of enemy that might one day be crafty enough to try to

divide before attempting to conquer. It is a holy state to be attained as an act of national piety, a sacred condition that mirrors not only the sublime unity of God on high, but also the equally marvellous interconnectedness of His various spheres and qualities. To serve the cause of Jewish unity, therefore, is to worship God.

How strange, then, to listen to those rabbis who speak nobly and loudly of their dedication to the cause, but who nevertheless proceed to destroy the unity of the Jewish people with their parochialism and formalism, with their self-serving arrogance, with their hostile denegation of any who dare disagree with them and with their provincial fundamentalism. To them all, a simple message: the Jewish people is not a patient that can survive having even one of its limbs amputated. To destroy the unity of Israel is to destroy Israel itself.

14. Leaven and Hell

Like three elderly aunties whirling around endlessly in a slightly demented dance of their own devising, the great pilgrimage festivals of ancient Israel live on in a cycle of festivals and holy days which doesn't quite accommodate them too well any longer.

The basic idea is that these holidays were originally the annual agricultural festivals of ancient Israel. Then, at a certain moment, they were historicized into the festive way-stations of Israel's annual re-enactment of the story of the Exodus from Egypt. (One can only assume that this process was intended to give those ancient holidays enough relevance beyond the borders of ancient Palestine to garner a permanent place for them in the affections of urban Jews who might no longer know the difference between a hoe and a rake, but who would always, presumably, value the concept of freedom and liberation from slavery for which these holidays were henceforth declared to stand.) Scripture seems to take both approaches at once, calling the holidays by different names in different contexts, some of which clearly reflect the agricultural festivals they originally were and others of which can only be explained in the context of the ancient story of Israel's escape from Egyptian bondage.

Passover, the festival celebrated as the anniversary of the actual exodus from Egypt itself, has the most going for it. Originally a festival connected with the spring grain harvest, it was first called the Matzah Festival, presumably after the dry crackers the labourers would eat in the fields during the harvest season when *shlepping* back to the manor house for meals would have meant taking too much time away from work. Afterwards, the matzah was recast in two only formally compatible ways, alternately serving as the latter-day model of the bread of affliction the Israelites are said to have eaten while they were slaves in Egypt and, a bit less plausibly, as what became of the un-pre-risen dough that the Israelites had to take along with them when the signal came in the middle of the night to pick up stakes and leave Egypt forever. The basic idea was a good one: the festivals of Israel are all designed to provide Jewish worshippers with a means of developing and demonstrating their faith in some specific quality or aspect of the God of Israel and Passover would henceforth be the holiday devoted to developing faith in the concept of God as the source of liberation. Now, even if they (mostly) aren't slaves in the formal sense, moderns have just as much need for liberation as our ancestors did. And so Passover was meant to provide the yearly opportunity to indoctrinate ourselves with precisely that aspect of our Jewish faith by giving us the opportunity to live within the myth of the Exodus, actually to *participate* in it as though we really were slaves in need of freedom and not just pathetic moderns enslaved to our own baser selves, to our own obstinacy, greed, stinginess, sloth and perverse desire to distance ourselves from the very God we claim we want nothing more than to encounter intimately and to love.

Unfortunately, the holiday hasn't weathered the test too well and has become the national festival of obsessive-compulsive behaviour rather than the festival of freedom it was originally designed to be. The desire to spend a week eating matzah instead of bread or other leavened cakes or cookies has been set aside in favour of an insane competition to see whose home can be even more entirely devoid of leaven or leavened products than his neighbours'. People use blow torches to eradicate the traces of *chometz* — the Hebrew term sounds so much more *repulsive* than its English equivalent — in their ovens. Others won't buy soda water if it hasn't been certified as kosher for Passover by one of the many rabbis who earn a fortune by selling such certification certificates to manufacturers anxious to corner the Passover market in Jewish neighbourhoods. (In Israel, I recall meeting people who don't drink tap water during Passover either, but I can't remember why not.) Vast sections of Jewry have even managed somehow to extend the prohibition to include rice, corn, peas and other kinds of legumes, vegetables that are somehow thought to be similar (when ground up into flour) to the kind of meal that can also be made into bread. People buy Passover jam and Passover tooth-paste and Passover lipsticks, Passover aspirin (which, believe me, you need) and Passover ketchup. In very Jewish neighbourhoods, there are even special springtime Passover supermarkets that carry exclu-sively Passover products so that the faithful can shop for the festival without having to fret about the ritual acceptability of their pur-chases.

At any rate, the whole point of the holiday — the worship of God as the source of all human liberation — is so completely buried under the endlessly compulsive effort to eradicate even the most suba-tomic trace of any leavened substance from our homes that the holiday has hardly any meaning at all in most settings and is merely pre-served as a convenient outlet for a winter's worth of manic energy. The tragedy of it all is that when more liberal families reject the kind of obsessive Passover preparation I've been describing, they almost never turn back wholeheartedly to the basic idea of cleaning the breads and cakes from their homes, replacing them with unleavened prod-ucts and using the experience as a spur to the worship of God as the great Liberator. Instead, they remain fixed on the holiday as they *don't* observe it and end up, mostly, with nothing too much at all except a box of matzah on their dinner table and a vague sense they shouldn't put it *right* next to the Twinkies in the cupboard when they clean up after their meal.

And yet, despite it all, there's still something very satisfying about Passover. No holiday is more evocative, more reminiscent of another age. No holiday brings Jewish people back into their parents' homes in a more satisfying way and no holiday is less likely to be overlooked, even by people who have no time for too much other formal Jewish observance. Perhaps the idea of liberation is so intensely satisfying that it simply can't be extinguished entirely. Perhaps the things that enslave us moderns — and not just nicotine and alcohol and pathological commercial acquisitiveness, either — are so horrifying when we contemplate the way they rule over us that we are simply too terrified *not* to acknowledge a God Who is presented to us as the source of freedom and liberation from them. We moderns are a pretty scared lot, I think. We wish to think of ourselves as being in control of our lives and our destinies, but we know that, mostly, we are completely out of control. We spend years developing excuses for our own inadequacies by discovering the ultimate reasons for our behaviour, but whether we seek solace in the fact that we are the slaves of our upbringings, of our hormones or our stormy adolescences, of our marriages or of our mortgage lenders, we do everything we can to convince ourselves that we have no real choices in our lives.

And then Passover comes and reminds us that there is one big choice left. We can seek liberation from all of the above — but only in the bosom of the God Who is the source of liberation and its inventor, the bestower of freedom on any and all who seek it in Him and its source. Perhaps that idea is so attractive to us all that, despite our best efforts, it simply refuses to die. So what can I say? The truth is that when I sit down at my own *seder* table on the eve of Passover and I recite the ancient words identifying the matzah as the bread of affliction, I can almost believe that I could be free. It seems outlandish — but even though I can hardly *really* believe it, the thought of being free of the chains that bind is so satisfying that I convince myself, yet again, that the holiday is not quite as bad as I thought while I was blow-torching the oven.

15. What the Moon Brought

When I was a boy, we had a book at home about the Jewish holidays called *What the Moon Brought*. I don't know what happened to it and I haven't seen a copy in years, although I believe the book is still in print, but it must have made a great impression on me because all my favourite Jewish rituals still have to do with the moon.

When I was younger and a lot more given to rituals of abstinence and atonement, I even used occasionally to fast on the eve of the New Moon, an old, now nearly defunct ritual of the Safed kabbalists designed to provide each month with a minor Day of Atonement just as the year had its major one on Yom Kippur. And even today, I still pronounce the mysterious benediction formally sanctifying the new moon on the first Saturday night of every Jewish month just after the end of the Sabbath. I don't know quite why it is that the moon has this effect on me — it's women who are supposed to be organized along the cycles of the moon, not men — but it does and, after all these years, I've finally shed my fear of saying so.

Maybe it has something to do with darkness itself. I've always liked the dark, even when I was a child and was supposed to be afraid once the lights went out and I was alone in my bed, eyes wide open and unable to see a thing. I can't explain it — I had all the other fears children are supposed to have — but I somehow liked the dark, liked the mystery of lightlessness and the sense that it held secrets that could possibly be coaxed from it by one brave enough to seek them out. I can remember taking physics in high school and learning that light was made up of photons (whatever they are) and thus an existent thing. Darkness, by contrast, we were taught is no thing at all, merely the absence of light. I understood the basic concept, but it seemed to go against my own experience. I liked light, I suppose, but it seemed hard to warm up to. Darkness, on the other hand, seemed very much to me to exist — and not merely as the absence of light. It had a feel and a texture and a context to it, a sort of pulse I fancied only I could feel, a rhythm I could hear if I stayed very still and allowed myself to be enveloped, not merely touched, but actually enshrouded and enwrapped in its obscure folds.

The contemplation of the dark brought me once to my first moment of prayer. I had been attending services in synagogue for many years and knew most of the liturgy well and many passages even by heart. I attended regularly and tried to say my prayers. I had even convinced myself that I prayed well, by which I meant that I understood the words (more than most worshippers can say!) and tried to say them with conviction and fervour. I had even convinced myself that I *liked* saying my prayers, liked the way the Hebrew words looked on the printed page, enjoyed the way they felt forming in my mouth and leaping out into the air to exist in whispered splendour for the briefest of moments before, I suppose I imagined, they whisked themselves off to heaven to present themselves before the God to whom they had been addressed.

In other words, I hadn't ever uttered a true word of prayer in my life, merely read what others had written for me at times others had stipulated for me to a God I knew only because those same liturgists and prayer-mavens had described Him to me.

This, however, was unknown to me at the time. I thought of myself as a good *davener*, even a pious practitioner of the art of Jewish prayer.

My in-laws used to own a cottage up in northeastern Ontario in a place called Jack Lake. It's an out of the way sort of place, not far from Lakefield, where Prince Andrew went to school briefly, and Peterborough, where Robertson Davies once worked as editor of the local newspaper. I spent parts of ten summers there, always enjoying the solitude and the sense that the world was both close and far away. It isn't even all that isolated a place, but it might as well have been — the nighttime sky was filled with the light of distant stars, but somehow the night there was still intensely dark and filled with the mystery and texture I could still remember from my bedroom in my parents' apartment when the light was switched off and the venetian blinds shut tight.

I used to go out at night and walk, secure I could find my way even though the darkness was so thick that it was impossible to navigate by even the most familiar landmarks. It wasn't *just* dark by the shores of Jack Lake, either. There was an almost viscous quality to the darkness, a sense that the dark was a shroud covering the world for the night and keeping it safe.

And there, one night all alone on a path I couldn't see, I discovered the meaning of prayer. I was out walking by myself, thinking about nothing more profound than how embarrassing it would be to fall into the lake and have to come back to the cottage soaking wet after everybody had *warned* me not to go out without a flashlight. Anyway, I was walking and thinking and wondering about things and then, for the first time ever, I felt the presence of God.

He didn't speak to me. He didn't vouchsafe me any good visions, either — no burning bushes, no chariot-thrones, no six-winged angels singing celestial hymns. He didn't grant me any information about the future either, and neither were there any secret revelations of the kind God is generally supposed to offer His faithful when He appears to them in the night. But that's just my point — He didn't appear at all to me. It wasn't He and I there on the path, it was just me.

But the me that stood there — and this only lasted for a few seconds — was transformed by the night, altered and transfigured by the sense that God was listening to me. I tried to think of something to say, some appropriate benediction to utter or some confession of faith that would sound right in such an unexpected moment.

My mind went blank. I, who had memorized such vast portions of the daily and Sabbath liturgies, couldn't think of a single thing to say. I thought of that awful story we rabbis are always citing about the little shepherd boy who was moved to prayer, but who knew none of the prayers in the prayerbook. He counted to ten, the story goes, because that was all he *could* do, and his prayer was as acceptable before the Almighty as the most involved, long-winded prayers of the greatest sages. I was actually considering counting to ten, when a single phrase popped into my head, the phrase from the evening liturgy in which God is acknowledged, almost in passing, as being the *maariv aravim*, the One Who causes evening to fall. It is such a banal idea, almost a throw-away line in one of the benedictions that precede the evening recitation of the *Hear O Israel* confession of Jewish faith that is the cornerstone of both the morning and the evening services. I had recited the phrase a thousand times, of course, but I had never really given it much thought and then, standing in the dark on the banks of Jack Lake, I understood just what it meant. The darkness was a shroud and, just for a moment, I was the lifeless body wrapped up in that black winding cloth. I stood at the boundary between life and death, between light and darkness, between good and evil. At the boundary between faith and disbelief, between creation and Creator.

I stood at a crossroads in my own life at that moment and, for the first time in my life, I understood what it meant to utter a word in prayer. It wasn't much — two words from a prayer somebody else once wrote — but for a moment, they formed a sort of metaphysical bridge that linked me to God. It was at that moment that I truly understood (and for the first time) that there was indeed a God and that I truly believed (also for the first time) that I wasn't crazy to devote myself to the propagation of a system of fealty and subservience to a God Whose existence I could neither prove nor argue. It was, even in retrospect, a great moment.

As the years have passed, I've had other moments in which I have felt the presence of God, not merely in an intellectual or even a spiritual way, but in a physical, tangible, visceral way that no one, not even I, could deny. For someone who tries to say his prayers three times every day, I'm a bit shy about admitting how few and far between these moments have been, although I'm not so naive as not to be slightly proud to have had any such moments at all.

God may have made the light and the light, as the book says, may well have been good. But for me, the experience of God is something to be sought and savoured in the dark, in the darkness of the night when the streets are quiet and the world is asleep. An ancient poet once wrote that we see light in the light of God's light, a phrase used liturgically every single morning of the year. I can't say that isn't true — probably, it *is* true — but, for me, "the blessings of God are only found in that which is hidden from the eye," in that which is enshrouded in darkness and hidden from the light.

16. Wrapped Up in Prayer

I think my oldest Jewish memory must be of sitting in synagogue on one of the High Holidays next to my father. He had — has — this enormous blue and white prayer shawl made of very smooth, very thick material and I would lean up against it and play with the fringes that hung down from it almost to the floor. All the men wore these shawls, called *tallesim* (one is called a *tallis* or, more often these days, a *tallit*), but they didn't all have the big kind that you can get all folded up and lost in. I knew even then that I was going to want the biggest one they made for myself once I was big enough to wear one.

In some synagogues, it's the custom for men only to wear a *tallit* once they get married. In our synagogue, however, the custom was to wear one after bar-mitzvah, but I had somehow failed to express my wishes clearly to my parents and had come through my bar-mitzvah experience with only a narrow *tallit* made of some sort of flimsy polyester — more of a scarf than a proper shawl — to my name. I didn't like my *tallit*, but I didn't want to hurt my parents' feelings and so I said nothing. And then, when we were both seventeen or eighteen, Laurie Edelman came back from Israel one summer with an enormous *tallit* for me as a gift. (She was a lot more pious than I was in those days — she still is — and I was only getting started in terms of my personal religious observance and this was sort of her welcome aboard present. It was extravagant and a bit surprising — in *her* circles, guys received their first big *tallit* as a wedding present just before they were married — but I was too much of a neophyte then even to *know* that and even if I had, I doubt I'd have cared much. It's still one of the best presents I've ever received from anybody.) I wear that *tallit* still. Every morning when I say my prayers. Every Sabbath and every festival in synagogue. The collar has been replaced a few times and I've tied new fringes on it once or twice, but the fabric itself is still intact, still large enough for me to wrap myself up in it while I say my prayers. It's not as thick or as smooth as my father's *tallit*, but you can hardly fix the value of things like prayer shawls based solely on the quality of the fabric from which they're fashioned. It's one of the only possessions I still have from my high school years and it's one I hope to keep my whole life. Even then some, actually, since it's our custom to bury men wearing their *tallesim* as well. I'm not looking forward especially to dying. But if I have to go someday, I want to go wearing the *tallit* Laurie brought for me when we were both teenagers back in Forest Hills.

A *tallit* is a funny sort of thing from a ritual point of view. Despite its world-wide recognition as a Jewish symbol (the flag of the State of Israel is patterned after a *tallit* held sideways with a Jewish star emblazoned in the middle), it has no real ritual role. The Torah commands us to fix fringes on our four-cornered garments as a means of remembering the commandments, but there's something odd about the whole situation: we wear the *tallit* because of the fringes, but one is required to wear the fringes only because one is wearing a *tallit* in the first place. Since the obligation to wear these fringes only falls upon one wearing a four-cornered garment, we could theoretically be free of the obligation to bother with the fringes merely by removing the four-cornered garment that requires them.

Since the Jewish practice is generally to observe the various commandments of Scripture as they naturally devolve upon us rather than to set up artificial situations in which to fulfill them, the only logical conclusion has to be that there must be some reason for wearing the *tallit* during prayers other than the simple self-necessitating point of *obliging* the wearer to don the requisite fringes.

And there is such a reason, but it's a bit poetic and has more than a hint of magic behind it: we don the *tallit* as an act of imitating the very God of Israel Himself Who donned a garment of light as He created the world and Who dons a garment woven of the collective souls of the Jewish people each morning as He prepares to receive and to harken unto the prayers of Israel.

There's another angle to consider as well: the *tallit* also symbolizes the soul of any individual that ascends to God during sleep and returns to revive the sleeper in the morning. Therefore, we don the *tallit* in the morning as a way of giving ritual reality to the gratitude any individual ought to feel towards the God Who has re-souled him and granted him his life anew, as we say in the liturgy every morning, "I give thanks to You, O living and existent God, for graciously having returned my soul unto me ..." This pious sense of beholdenness and gratitude in turn works its own magic: it inspires, or it is supposed to inspire, God Himself to don His own garment, not the garment of light He wore as He created the world, but the special soul-cloak He is to wear to bring about the final redemption.

That cloak, described in so many different ways in different liturgical and mystical contexts, is the key to the redemption of Israel, its symbol and its agent. The Jewish people, taken as a collective whole, act as the soul of God, returning unto Him each morning in prayer and thanksgiving just as the soul of each individual Jewish man or woman returns to him or her each morning as a sign of God's enduring love. When the gratitude Israel feels towards its God finally approaches the love God feels for Israel, then the moment of the final redemption will possibly have come.

As for us down here, we have no real choice but to continue wrapping on our own soul-cloaks, donning our own prayer shawls morning after morning to create and perfect the spiritual world on earth just as God once donned his own cloak of light to create the physical universe in which we live.

The years have passed. Laurie married Harvey, moved to Jerusalem and had five children. I married Joan, had three children and ended up as the rabbi of a synagogue in British Columbia. The *tallit* is on my shelf in our synagogue's sanctuary, wrapped in a piece of purple velvet my mother sewed for it as she lay dying. It's just a piece of black and white cloth with some strings hanging from its corners, but it's somehow become the focus of a lot of vectors in my life: my ties to the scenes of my childhood in New York and to Jerusalem (where my eldest son was born), my memories of my late mother and, *yibadel lechayyim arukhim*, my father whom I still see wrapped up in that ancient *tallit*, thick and smooth with its iridescent blue stripes, my faith in the ancient creation and the coming redemption and in the God Who is Redeemer and Creator and Restorer of Souls, the God to Whom I pray and regarding Whose existence I pray and Whose presence I hope someday to feel as deeply again as when I was a boy snuggled up against my father in synagogue as he contemplated God and I contemplated him.

17. All Alone By Myself

People are supposed to hate being alone. I'm guilty of falling into that trap myself: when people confide to me that they prefer their own company to the company of others, I usually try to find some gentle way to recommend some sort of professional therapy that might help the individual in question find his or her way back into society. And I'm hardly alone in feeling that way: people who like to be alone are suspect in our world, as though the preference of one's own company must necessarily be the special trait of egotists, loiterers or compulsive masturbators. But whether we are children who make fun of such people or adults who sympathetically try to help them, the fact remains that society considers people who cultivate solitude to be unhappy, troubled souls who have lost their connection to the world.

But solitude is not the same as aloneness, or rather it is precisely the same, but we *call* it solitude when the individual involved is respected rather than pitied for his predilection for his own company. Some Jewish authors — Abraham Maimuni, the son of Maimonides, among them — have written eloquently, even persuasively, about the way of solitude as the most basic path towards communion with God. Their works, however, are rarely read and often misquoted and misunderstood as being in opposition to the more regular rabbinic insistence on the need for community and fellowship in the worship of God. But there's something in what Maimuni writes, something deep and profoundly acceptable about his insistence that the path to God lies through a desert one must traverse alone.

There's an old Buddhist book by a Mahayana author known as Shantideva that I read years ago while I was in rabbinical school. In it, he talks warmly about the need any religious individual ought to feel to be alone in his or her quest for union with God, talking about "delightful and untroubled solitude/bestowing bliss and stilling all distractions". I don't know why Shantideva's poetry made such an impression on me when I read it, but it did and I can quote it still.

Most of us do not know solitude to be delightful and untroubled. Just to the contrary, most of us know it to be painful and lonely. We avoid being alone at all costs, preferring to leave solitude for those who cannot avoid it and those few mystics who are willing to undergo it in order to attain the higher spheres. But the liturgy is filled with hints that this state of utter aloneness is not only the province of the saints, but the state to which all must aspire if their personal quests for union and communion with God are to end successfully.

If that is the case, then Jewish tradition must be truly perverse with its almost constant harping on the need for community. (The one who separates himself from the community is held up not so much for ridicule as for scorn by the rabbis and is penalized by being denied the right to recite the most sacred sections of the prayer service in the absence of nine other worshippers.) The stance is basic: the rabbis presumed that Abraham bargained God down to sparing Sodom if there were ten righteous souls living there — ten, but not fewer than ten — because they presume Abraham couldn't possibly have conceived of a situation in which righteous people would have agreed in the first place to live in a place where there were too few to form a proper quorum for prayer.

As a rabbi, I try to synthesize these basically incompatible values, but I don't do a very good job, I don't think. We encourage communal prayer at the same time we know that prayer is among the most intensely private acts there is. We encourage people to organize synagogues, knowing full well that the path to knowing God is a lonely journey that can *only* be taken alone. We tell people that the tools of communion with God are scrolls and books and prayer shawls and phylacteries, knowing that the paraphernalia of worship can just as easily diminish as enhance the chances of experiencing the presence of God.

We are a singular people embarked on a singular path towards God. We journey alone together towards Jerusalem, weary pilgrims on a lonely pilgrimage hoping to find a respite from the loneliness in the company of other lonely people. We do seek God together, but we do so hoping that the company of like-minded people might provide the impetus to pursue the journey each of us knows must ultimately be made alone. At prayer, we form prayer quorums so as to travel in a group along the path each of us must travel alone. For, in the final analysis, the path to God is different for each of us, just as the nature and quality of love experienced is different for every human heart.

Long ago, there was a magic kingdom so vast that there was a separate magic forest in it for each individual citizen to explore and enjoy. And the magic of these forests lay in this: the paths in each single forest were all magically interconnected so that no matter how far in any one direction a citizen might absent-mindedly walk, the path he was travelling eventually brought him to the destination he had had in mind upon entering the forest. However, since no wanderer ever met another in the forest that was designated for his sole use, this fact went unnoticed and its implications unconsidered for many generations. Eventually, of course, the citizenry grew so large that this arrangement could no longer be continued and two citizens were assigned the same magic forest in which to wander. As time passed, the numbers increased until each forest became crowded with wanderers and hikers. Although the magic nature of the forest stopped once the citizens began to ponder the impossible physics involved in a forest in which all the paths led automatically to the precise spot each individual wanderer was seeking on any particular visit, some vestigial remnant of the ancient wonder lingered on in this: the paths that had led those who trod them to their desired destinations now only led those who wandered them deeper and deeper into the primeval forest. As there were now no paths out at all, the citizenry began to diminish as countless numbers of wanderers disappeared into the kingdom's vast forests never to be heard from again. When the citizenry was finally shrunk down to its original size, the kingdom returned to its former practice of assigning each individual citizen his or her own forest to explore. The magic returned immediately, but, of course, no one noticed ...

18. A Bloody Bridegroom

Do you remember the story of Moses' trip back to Egypt once the time had finally come for him to lead his people to freedom? He had been living in Midian for a long, long time when he was finally told by God that the people who had been planning to kill him were themselves dead — he had gotten himself into a rough situation by killing an Egyptian who had been torturing an Israelite slave — and that it was now safe for him to go back to his brethren and save them from Egyptian bondage.

So what did he do? He packed up his bags and he saddled up his donkeys and he and Zipporah and their boys, Gershom and Eliezer, set out for the journey back to Egypt. So at first, the journey is uneventful, but then something bizarre and amazing happens. It's nighttime and Zipporah is sitting up on guard while Moses is asleep. Then, suddenly God Himself appears and begins to wrestle with Moses. Now Zipporah was no fool, but she just doesn't know what to do. Who could have known? But Moses' life is in danger and she has to do *something*.

So the angel Gabriel looks down on the scene and he knows, somehow, that he alone is in a position to save the day. But what exactly can he do — angels are only allowed to speak to human beings when God allows it. Still, Gabriel knows there must be a way and, eventually, he figures out what it must be. So he comes down to earth and finds the camp and there, sure enough, are God and Moses rolling around in the dirt and wrestling with each other. Gabriel tries to figure out how to tell Zipporah what to do without actually speaking to her when, suddenly, God releases Moses for a second to let him get his breath before the next round.

And that's when Gabriel sees his chance. He turns himself into a snake and begins to swallow Moses up alive. First he swallows his head, then his shoulders and arms, then he bends his legs up around his back and swallows them too until only Moses' penis is visible.

Now here is where I have a problem with the commentators. They all say that Zipporah gets a load of this picture — and it must have been *some* picture — and she suddenly understands that Moses is going to die because he hadn't bothered to circumcise their son Eliezer. She understands that and then she has the idea to pick up a rock — a flint of the kind you find in the desert — and to cut off the boy's foreskin then and there and to fling it at Moses' feet, which she does, exclaiming, "Behold you are a bridegroom of blood to me!" As well he was, at least at that point.

But here is my problem: why wouldn't Moses have circumcised his boy when the child was an infant? And if he didn't circumcise Eliezer for some reason, then why *would* he have circumcised Gershom? And if he didn't circumcise Gershom either, then why did God let him go after Zipporah only circumcised Eliezer? You see the problem ...

At any rate, I have my own theory, which is that the Torah is being delicate here. The rabbis said the Torah always goes out of its way to be delicate, especially when some sensitive point is being discussed. (And what could be more sensitive than this particular issue?) So what I think is that Zipporah circumcised Moses himself with her flint and that the story doesn't have anything to do with the boys at all. Here's how I figure: of course, Moses would have circumcised his sons. Why wouldn't he have? He wasn't in Egypt where Pharaoh might have found out. He was in his father-in-law's home and Jethro was a *mensch* who later proved himself to be a good friend of the Jewish people. But even if Jethro hadn't been a good guy, it's still unthinkable that Moses would have forgotten about giving his sons a proper circumcision. Besides, if it was his son's *bris* that was lacking, then why did Gabriel gobble up Moses and not the boy? And there's more — if it was the boy that wasn't circumcised, why does Zipporah say afterwards that doing the deed made *Moses* her bridegroom of blood? Certainly she doesn't mean that her little boy is her bridegroom. (Although one ancient rabbi, presumably equally perplexed by the story, actually insists that is precisely what she meant.)

If you ask me, the clear meaning is that Moses is the uncircumcised one. And it makes sense — why would *his* parents have circumcised *him*? He was the one who was born when Pharaoh was out to kill all the Jewish boys in Egypt, so it seems reasonable to assume that the last thing his parents would have wanted was to make it obvious that their son was Jewish. Besides, if they hid him for three months with the intention of putting him in the basket and sending him down the Nile, then for sure they wouldn't ruin the whole thing by circumcising him — they might as well have just carved the word Jew on Baby Moses' forehead.

So that's why I think it was Moses who needed the operation and it was Zipporah who gave it to him. Of course *Moses* is the bridegroom — who else should be his wife's bridegroom? And of course that is why Gabriel swallowed him alive, until only his uncircumcised penis was sticking out of the angel's mouth.

Still, there are some problems with my explanation. For instance, let's go back to the part about Moses probably not having been circumcised as an infant. True, his parents were undoubtedly afraid to circumcise him and there certainly are times when it is right not to do a *mitzvah*, for instance when you would be risking a human life by doing it. But there's still a problem — our Torah teaches that a parent is only obliged to circumcise a boy until the child is a barmitzvah. After thirteen years of age, the responsibility is the boy's — or, after his bar-mitzvah, I should say the man's — alone.

Now Moses was 120 years old when he died, so when he led the Israelites out of Egypt, he must have been eighty. So the job had been his to do for a very long time when he and Zipporah were travelling from Midian to Egypt, but my theory has to assume that he hadn't done it and I don't know why. God apparently didn't understand why not either, which is why he decided to get his attention by wrestling him to the ground in the middle of the night.

So God tried to get him, but Gabriel and Zipporah knew what to do. God does that a lot — setting up situations just to let mortals show their mettle even though He must know the outcome in advance. Maybe the proof that I'm right is that God was wrestling with Moses in the first place. God doesn't *have* to wrestle people to the ground to get their attention, you know. If God wanted Moses dead, he could have killed him with a word, just like Moses killed the Egyptian who was beating up the Israelite, but He didn't really want him dead — he wanted Zipporah to circumcise him and that she did, flinging his foreskin at her husband's feet and saying, "There you are, you bloody bridegroom. Next time, do it yourself and leave me out of it!"

I think a lot about Moses and God rolling in the dust in the dark, cold night. But mostly I think about Zipporah. Did she realize Moses' attacker was God Himself? I doubt it. How then did she realize what to do? And how did she know this particular snake who was devouring her husband was an angel in disguise? It must have been a question of size — after all, if the snake ate Moses alive, it must have been one enormous serpent.

So here is the scene as I see it now: the night is dark and cold and suddenly a man starts wrestling with Moses, wakening him from his sleep and dragging him outside of his tent. Suddenly, when they break to catch their breaths, a giant serpent appears and gobbles up Moses until only his penis is hanging right out of the snake's mouth and flopping down across the snake's ribbed belly.

Then: satori! The scales fall from Zipporah's eyes and she suddenly sees the situation for what it is. She grabs a sharp flint from the ground and slices off her husband's foreskin, whereupon the snake pukes him out onto the ground and slithers off, we can only presume, into the desert night. But Zipporah isn't quite through: she flings the foreskin at her husband and says her mysterious words, but the point is that Moses was about to die for his laxity and his wife saved him with her flint.

Jewish law specifically permits women to act as *mohalot*, as circumcisers of Jewish infant boys, but it just hasn't been our practice for a couple of thousand years to allow women to exercise that entirely legal and licit prerogative. I personally think the moment has come for some new thinking in this regard ...

19. Chimneys and Churches

I think maybe the hardest thing for non-Jews to understand about Jews and Judaism is that we are not a missionary faith, not a nation of doorbell ringers and tract hander-outers, not a people devoted to getting other people to become what we ourselves are. To me it all seems quite natural and normal, but for outsiders, especially Christian outsiders, the whole idea appears to be almost incomprehensible. "If you value your own faith, why don't you want to share it with others?" is the polite way they put their question when I speak to non-Jewish groups. It's a nice way to put it, but what they're really saying is that the imperialist slant of their own religious agenda is so deeply woven into the fabric of who *they* are and what *they* believe about the nature of religion that they simply (and innocently) can't fathom what it would mean for somebody to say that he finds his own beliefs and practices deeply satisfying and spiritually rewarding, but that he doesn't just assume *a priori* that everybody in the world is *supposed* to share them.

I've been canvassed by the best of them. For years, I received mail from missionary organizations that wanted me to know the truth about Jesus. I *still* get New Testaments in the mail by the dozen from complete strangers concerned for the state of my eternal soul. (I have a shelf in my library with *nothing* but unsolicited copies of the New Testament on it, including three or four *different* Hebrew-language editions. Presumably, seeing the gospels translated into Hebrew is somehow expected to cut through years of my stubborn Jewish rejectionism and finally get me to acknowledge truth that ought to have been self-evident in the first place.) Needless to say, this is all a one-way street and if Jews began targeting innocent Christians and bombarding them with pamphlets denigrating Christianity as malign or trivial and insisting that *their* only path to salvation lay through their local synagogue, we'd be widely condemned as fanatics and maniacs who have completely failed to seize the essentially non-coercive nature of religion in a multicultural democracy.

But, since the unabashed, openly stated goal of the missionary organizations involved is the annihilation of Judaism and Jewish life, it's hard for me to explain away missionary activity as nothing but a combination of excessive zeal and thoughtlessly directed religious fervour. Still, I am prepared to make one (small) concession and that is I have come to believe that the whole *idea* of missionary work is *so* deeply embedded in the consciousness and world view of at least some Christians that they can hardly be expected to hold themselves back. (These are the same people, incidentally, who are simply *amazed* when told that Jews resent missionary activity. They sugarcoat it with all the nicest names — bringing the good news to the nations, evangelizing the world, stuff like that — but missionary work, most simply put, is by definition an attempt to demolish the religious culture and spirituality of any non-Christian group that has the temerity to continue to exist in the world now that the only real religion is available for their spiritual consumption. When I speak forcefully in some interfaith forum about the need for Christians to abandon their missionary activity, somebody in the audience *always* stands up to profess utter shock that Christendom's noble efforts to save us all are being met with such unremitting hostility. Sorry about the hostile tone, folks — but Judaism ends up pretty much just as extinct whether the former Jews end up in chimneys or in churches. I hate to put it so bluntly, but there it is: if you want me to respect you, stop trying to destroy my people and my faith. Period.)

At any rate, the point is for me to try to explain why it is that Jews *aren't* missionaries, not why Christians are. Needless to say, we *do* value our faith, *do* indeed consider it a worthy road towards salvation, *do* believe Judaism to be an effective vehicle towards communion with God. So why don't I think everybody should adopt our way?

For one thing, our own faith teaches us otherwise.

The Bible lays down some few rules that everybody should follow. These rules, the so-called seven commandments given to the sons of Noah, are mostly norms of societal and human decency: not to murder or steal, not to torture animals, to set up a system of courts and judges — that sort of stuff. But none of them is going to help anyone achieve the kind of spiritual communion with God that is the common spiritual goal of all religious people. That, Torah implies tacitly, is their problem to solve.

Every nation, we are left to presume, has its own nature. That much certainly seems to be true. Nations, left on their own, develop different cuisines, different kinds of music and dance, different styles of literature, even different modes of dress. The thing is that, although everybody knows these things to be so, nobody can really explain them in any rational way. Everyone, for example, knows that the Japanese eat sushi and the Italians eat pasta and the Indians eat curries. That much is obvious, but when you ask why — what *precisely* it is about sushi that corresponds so profoundly to something deep within the collective national soul of the Japanese that it becomes the gastronomic *symbol* of the nation — no one is quite prepared to say. That it corresponds to *something* is obvious, but identifying that something and explaining how the correspondence works *exactly* — that, no one seems quite able to do.

Religion is the same way, I think. There are many nations, but only one God. Each people on earth, therefore, has the task of somehow groping towards God, of developing a means of spiritual expression that will correspond to something so deeply embedded within the national ethos that the spiritual quest becomes somehow assimilated to the destiny of the people in question. Now here is the point that will amaze my Christian readers: I have no problem with this. In fact, I wish the peoples of the world would *renew* their dedication to their own spiritual paths. I don't think everybody is supposed to be Jewish and, truth be told, I'm always slightly amazed when a non-Jew approaches me about conversion to Judaism.

It's true that we do accept converts. But reluctantly. Even *very* reluctantly. And only after we've done our best to talk the perspective convert out of proceeding with the whole idea. Now, it's also true that once we do allow somebody to convert to Judaism, they are considered Jewish in the fullest sense of the word. But that's only after they complete their conversions. Before that, there's no pressure, no coercion, not even too much overt encouragement. As a rabbi who does accept prospective converts as pupils, I walk a narrow line trying to be my students' teacher and spiritual leader for as long as they pursue their studies without ever suggesting that I'm actually hoping they decide to convert to Judaism at the end of our course of study. I like my students and I feel for their spiritual longings, but I have to discipline myself *not* to care if they convert or not. At the end of the day, the decision has to be theirs and theirs alone because only they can say whether, through some remarkable quirk of circumstance, the Jewish system of ritual and faith actually works for them or not. The point is that I don't *expect* it to work for anybody but born Jews. For better or worse, Judaism belongs to the Jewish people. We invented it, we perfected it, we've been working on it for four thousand years or so. With all its quirks and warts, it belongs to us and, although we are prepared to share it with those occasional few who wish to join us, it doesn't necessarily seem likely that it will suit anybody but us.

Why is that? What is it about Judaism that corresponds so deeply to the spiritual longing of Jewish individuals? That may be the sixty-four thousand dollar question, but the simple answer is that I haven't the faintest idea. Ask the Japanese why they eat sushi better. Or maybe God did invent all the religions of the world and parcel them out to the appropriate peoples. Could the Jews be the chosen people — chosen for Judaism, that is — after all?

20. Believing is Seeing

Everybody knows that the idea of faith is central to any religious system; this is so much the case that we actual use the word "faith" to mean "religion" as though that were all there was to it. But Judaism has always prided itself on being different and, for Jews, deeds have always counted more than mere thoughts or convictions. The commandments were to be *done*, not merely (merely!) believed in — and this was so much the case that even those of the commandments of Scripture that *appeared* to be doable in a purely intellectual way were reinterpreted by the rabbis to require at least *some* slight physical act. So the rabbis taught that even the famous fourth of the Ten Commandments could not be fulfilled merely by *remembering* that the seventh day of the week was the Sabbath, although that is precisely what Scripture commands. Instead, a formal liturgy of sanctification was composed to be recited over a cup of wine (or, in a pinch, over a loaf of bread), the recitation of which constituted the only legitimate means of fulfilling that commandment.

But the matter isn't quite that simple. Serving God with one's spirit, doing the ritual acts of one's faith within the confines of the intellect, merely *believing* in God as one's sole act of worship — these may not be enough, but faith itself is still as basic to Judaism as it is to any religion. And the catalyst that transforms Judaism from a motley collection of superstitious rites and shamanistic warding-off rituals into worship of the most elevated order is indeed faith. Faith in God. Faith in the God of Israel.

I don't know what everybody else thinks, but I think that faith is a difficult thing. Believing in God is not to be confused with declaring one's faith in God or even in behaving *as though* one believed in God wholeheartedly. Believing in God is just that: perceiving the world in such a way that you can no more imagine that there might not be a God than you would seriously argue that there is no such thing as gravity. Now that kind of faith does not come from simply wishing to have it and neither can it be acquired by praying for it. (And, at any rate, to whom would you address the prayer?) Faith comes only through years and years of effort, of trying to *use* the rituals and rites of Judaism as techniques to bring oneself to a state of intense faith in God.

If I were to stop any random number of people on the street and ask if they believed in God, I suppose that some would say they did and others would say they didn't and still others, probably the majority, would say that they weren't sure. Now, if one of them were to turn the tables on me and ask if *I* believed in God, I would say that I do believe — but that is only because I think that would probably be the honest answer to the question that person probably meant to ask. But the real answer is more difficult and more complex. Belief in God isn't a yes/no proposition; it is a process that lasts a lifetime and which takes us over the decades of our lives to a state in which God's existence becomes truly axiomatic.

As I'm writing this, I can see a man walking his dog just across the street. Now I don't know this man, don't know his name or his occupation, don't know where he's from or what he's like or whether he's married or has children. In fact, I don't know anything at all about him except that he is wearing a grey overcoat and, presumably, owns the beagle that is chewing on my neighbour's flowerbed. That's it.

Still, if you were to try to talk me into believing that this fellow across the street doesn't exist, that the beagle is walking down the street unescorted by anybody, that his leash is simply floating up towards the sky as the result of some bizarre gravitational anomaly, I'd laugh at your efforts. In other words, here is some man I don't know, about whom I could not conceivably know any less and whom

I have no particular interest in getting to know — and yet, everything I know about the universe — about eyesight and perspective, about gravity and the habits of dogs, about the way people perceive things by observing the world around them — these and a thousand other things *require* that I believe with all my heart that this man across the street is standing there and existing. But if you ask me about God, my answer is different. I've come a long way since I began this Jewish journey of mine. I started with almost no real faith and through decades of religious observance and prayer I've come to believe. But if you were to argue with me that the man across the street isn't there, I'd have to assume you were either being insincere or else that you were demented in some serious way. Is my faith in the God I've tried to serve all these years *that* certain? Would I — do I — assume that people who don't believe in God are necessarily crazy? Can I conceive of the fact that I might be wrong and the naysayers be right, a proposition I don't think I could seriously entertain regarding the dog walker across the street?

The answer is ... not yet. I've grown in my faith and I'm pleased by my growth. But I'm not *that* old yet and I hope to live a long life. If I thought my faith had already grown to its fullest flower, I'd find that a very depressing thought indeed.

The point of Judaism is the worship of God in the context of love. But love is predicated on knowledge, just as knowledge is predicated on faith. Now we spend our lives trying to develop faith, for without faith there can be no knowledge and without knowledge, no love. But we know almost nothing about faith, not how to engender it and not how to nurture it. We don't know where it comes from or where it goes to when we wake up one day and find it missing. We have spent thousands of years now trying to devise methods and techniques to develop our faith. Some of our ways have become famous, while others remain unknown or almost unknown outside the walls of our own synagogues. Some of these methods have enjoyed universal acceptance while others have been accepted by some and not others. Some have become so central to our Jewish way of life that rejecting them has come to be impossible for those who would remain part of the organized Jewish community, while others, for all their theoretical requiredness, remain optional and are chosen by some and not by others. These techniques are the commandments of the Torah, the procedures our ancestors considered so effective in establishing the intimate state of communion which is the goal of Jewish life and effort that they could only assume they were inspired by God Himself, a God as anxious to be loved as He is ready to love.

And perhaps that is precisely the point. Perhaps God has indeed given us the commandments by inspiring us to develop and formulate them so that, through them, we might come to believe wholeheartedly and unreservedly in Him. Then those who see the Bible as a work of human hands *and* those who insist that Scripture is a revelation from God would both be right. And *that* vituperative debate set aside, Jewish people from all schools of thought could join together to build the faith that is the point of the whole endeavour in the first place. Faith is not for children and neither is the quest for faith an undertaking for the fainthearted. It is the sublime agent that transforms superstition into ritual and magic into religion, the transcendental enzyme that transforms human beings into creatures of God.

21. December

I can't stand Christmas. Call me Grinch, call me Scrooge, call me whatever you want — but leave me out of it. Now don't misunderstand, I have no problem with Christians observing Christian holidays. In fact, I'm strongly in *favour* of Christians observing Christian holidays. I just don't want those holidays crammed down my throat the way Christmas is every December whether my gullet is ready or not. And don't tell me Christmas *isn't* really a religious holiday, so I'm all in a dither about nothing. I agree they've ruined it. If I *were* a Christian, I'm sure I'd hate the crass commercialism, the almost inconceivable greed and acquisitiveness the holiday generates, the way Santa and Rudolf have shoved Jesus out of the spotlight in so many different settings. I'm sure I'd hate having the most sacred day of my year reduced to jingles and store-bought eggnog and endless strings of little coloured lights.

But, you say, I'm *not* a Christian, so it's not my problem. Wrong again — it's my problem because they won't leave me out of it. My *bank* has a Christmas tree every December and all the tellers spend the month wishing all the customers a merry Christmas. (How actually should I respond to *that*? Should I spit in their faces? Inform them frostily that I shall have no Christmas at all, thank you very much? Or should I just pass — just mumble back an inaudible Merry Christmas and pass, just that one little time, for one of them? After all, why shouldn't I deny my own identity and heritage for the sake of not appearing ungrateful for a thoughtless remark designed to make me feel like a stranger in my own bank?)

I can't stand any of it — Rudolf and Santa and the lights and the phoney-baloney good will on earth thing. You want good will? Can the tinsel and stuff the stockings, put your religion back in your churches and leave the public arena safe for people who don't share your religious beliefs to enter without being made to feel like outsiders. And have a very merry Christmas ... if there's enough fun left in the holiday once you've stopped using it as a whip to crack over the backs of us infidels once a year. We promise — we'll know our place anyway!

Let me hasten to assure you, however, that I am an equal-opportunity spoilsport: I don't like Chanukah either. I don't dislike it as much as Christmas, but I don't like it that much either. I don't like what we've done to it or what we allow other people to do to it. I don't like Chanukah being allowed to pass as the Jewish Christmas, which it isn't, or as the celebration of the success of armed resistance to tyranny, which it also isn't. You see, I know the real story of Chanukah, the one we've been repressing for a couple of thousand years. Come around, children, and Daddy will tell you the story of Chanukah, the real story, depressing and upsetting as you may find it ...

Once upon a time, there was a man who ruled the world. His name was Alexander and he really did manage to conquer more or less all he knew of the planet — a feat that has eluded even his most successful successors in the world dominion arena. He lived and died and his kingdom ended up divided among his various generals and aides-de-camp. Of course, they couldn't quite decide *how* to divide up the spoils and they ended up fighting, but when the dust finally settled, the land of Israel was in the part of Alexander's empire that was ruled by the descendants of one Seleucus, the general who had centred his base of operation in Syria. Neither Seleucus nor his successors on the Seleucid throne (all of whom, for some maddening, if obscure, reason were named Antiochus) were real Syrians, of course. They were Greeks and their culture was Greek culture, or rather the hybrid of Oriental and Greek ideas known by moderns as Hellenism.

Hellenism wasn't just a philosophy, however; it was a way of life, a set of basic cultural ideas that permeated society. The best modern parallel would be the way we use the term Western Civilization to refer to the set of underlying ideas that provide the *framework* for the cultural details that characterize the world we have constructed for ourselves here in the West. But this was something new when it appeared on the scene: the idea of a multinational, world-wide culture was something nobody had ever experienced before. Nowadays, Jews are semi-good at picking out the parts of Western culture that are inimical to traditional Jewish life (Santa Claus and the Easter bunny come to mind) and distinguishing them from the parts that are benign (like baseball) or even desirable (like safe sex). But then, back in the second and third centuries B.C.E., nobody had any experience at all in this. And as a result, the Jews weren't very good at figuring out what parts of outside culture were basically importable into Jewish life and which parts really were cancers destined to destroy the parts of Jewish life with which they came into contact.

As is our usual custom, the Jews split into warring factions. Both parties went crazy, driven to extremes by an intoxicating brew of naiveté, insecurity, inexperience and fanaticism. The Hellenists among the Jews didn't know how to stop at enjoying Aeschylus, Sophocles and Euripides — they wanted to abandon circumcision and incorporate the worship of Greek gods into Jewish practice and give up everything about Judaism that they deemed particularist and xenophobic. The more orthodox types were also inclined to pitch out the baby with the bath water. They rejected Hellenism completely and wanted none of it — no sports, no theatres, no philosophy, no nothing. They wanted Jewish civilization to remain what they felt it had always been — an insulated haven safe from alien ideas, foreign practices and extrinsic innovation.

Since nobody could see eye to eye, they went to war. And that's the ugly secret about Chanukah that nobody tells — that the war the Maccabees won (the Maccabees were the guerilla champions of the xenophobes) was basically a civil war. True, the Seleucid king came to the aid of the Hellenist party and sent his best general, a fellow named Nicanor, into the fray on their behalf. And also true that he enacted legislation designed to strengthen the hands of that same side. But we sin against history when we allow ourselves to remember the whole episode as one of a foreign king's attempt to destroy Judaism instead of as a civil war between warring Jewish factions in which one side profited from foreign intervention and one side didn't.

We've been doing our best to falsify the data for at least two thousand years, but a few of us still read enough to know the truth. The story we tell the children about the brave Maccabees and the lonely little cruse of oil that burned for eight days instead of one is a good tale, but it's a bit of a fairy story. So no, Virginia, Chanukah is not the Jewish Christmas, even if the Jewish and Christian worlds have done their best to ruin them both by doing whatever they could to guarantee that their real messages be buried under enough gift-wrap to smother even the most interesting realities.

22. Ehud

Like any student of the Bible, I have my favourite books and passages. It's hard to choose one over the others, but I think that if I had to name the book of the Bible I like the most, it would have to be the Book of Judges.

It's a shame no one ever reads it. I mean, *some* people must read it, but it isn't a big draw for Bible study groups or for most private admirers of the ancient text. Lacking the poetry of Isaiah, the pathos of Jeremiah, the majesty of the Psalms and deep wisdom of Proverbs or Ecclesiastes, Judges sort of gets grouped with its sister books of early Israelite history as filler material commissioned, one can only presume, by some ancient publisher to move the reader along from the time of Moses to the reigns of Saul, David and Solomon. Which is too bad, since the book has its own appeal and speaks directly to me in a way the later history books don't.

Even before I learned the word, what I liked the most about Judges was its nihilism.

After completing the conquest of the Land of Israel, the Israelites somehow resisted the temptation to set up a central government. The fact that in the days of the prophet Samuel, the last and greatest judge of them all, they finally did give in and demand a king to rule over them has little to do with it — what matters to me is that for long generations, the Jews resisted the urge to be governed at all. Instead, they simply lived in peace, rousing themselves to rally around some pivotal figure like Deborah or Gideon from time to time when some group or another of marauding *goyim* threatened to disturb the tranquillity of the Holy Land.

Having spent all of my life in countries that are horrendously over-governed, the thought that Israel somehow managed to establish itself in its own land without any *apparatchiks* at all gnawing at the fabric of their society seems almost impossible to imagine. Yet the account of just that situation is available in the Book of Judges for all to read. The final verse in the book, for example, which was meant (I suppose) in a negative sense by its author, has always spoken directly to me: "In those days, there was no king in Israel; everyone did as he thought right." For a long time, those Hebrew words, *ish hayashar be'enav yaaseh*, were my private motto. They were my favourite doodle too — I remember filling up margin after margin of the newspaper with them (as though I could somehow make them my own by copying them out enough times) while sitting through those endless lectures that constituted most of my undergraduate education.

I've always felt an especially strong sense of kinship with the minor figures in the book, the characters no one has ever heard of. In fact, when I've dreamt of figures from Judges, it's invariably been those obscure heroes of ungoverned Israel that have been the central figures in my dreams.

For example, I have this recurring dream about Ehud ben Gera, the second of Israel's judges. Ever hear of him? Don't worry if you haven't — his story is as brief as it is obscure. But brevity and obscurity can't take his claim to fame from him — Ehud ben Gera was the fellow who took on King Eglon of Moab and won.

Eglon means Little Ox and his name was well chosen; when Ehud plunged a dagger precisely one *gomed* long into the king's right side, the rolls of royal fat closed over both the blade and its hilt. In my dream, Eglon of Moab is always as immensely fat as a sumo wrestler, always naked, always caught by surprise while rising from his sumptuous privy stool to hear the message from God that Ehud claims he has come to reveal.

The Bible, I admit, only says that Ehud approached the king when he was sitting in his cool upper chamber, but it's obvious that the chamber has to have been a privy because it turns out later that

Ehud was able to escape precisely because the king's servants were unwilling to disturb their master during his visit there. So in my dream, I can see King Eglon seated in imperial dignity on his ruby-studded ivory toilet, his satin and velvet robes tossed carelessly onto one of the various jaguar-skin rugs that are lying in planned disarray on the cold golden floor. I can see the king sitting on his hollow ivory throne when Ehud comes in, his lack of shame regarding his own nakedness the ultimate sign of disdain for the Israelite lad whom he has allowed to come in to amuse him (while he can't get up any-way) with a self-proclaimed message from the God of Israel. And I can see the king's eyes bulge open in disbelief when Ehud draws his double-edged dagger and rams it into the king's enormous, white side.

Just as the Bible specifically says one who was there would have had to, I can actually see the fecal filth leaking out of the king's pierced bowel. It's a bit grotesque, but the image that stays with me is that of the dagger disappearing entirely into the king's fat so that all the onlooker can see is excrement oozing out as though from some hideously misplaced cloaca.

Is the specific point of the narrative to stress how the overpowering odour of the king's feces was responsible for keeping his attendants-in-waiting all too aware that the king was not yet ready to be disturbed? Or did the Biblical author describe the king of Moab lying dead, naked and covered in his own dirt only because it was the ultimate insult of which he could conceive? I don't know, but I still love the story. To cite a different one of Israel's judges, so may all the enemies of Israel perish!

But it's not only Ehud ben Gera with whom I feel such a sense of kinship. For his name alone, I like Tola ben Puah ben Dodo, no detail of whose twenty-three years as judge was deemed of sufficient interest to warrant incorporation into Scripture. And I like the virile symmetry of a man like Yair the Gileadite, whose thirty sons owned thirty villages and rode on thirty donkeys, only to be outdone by Ibzan of Bethlehem who not only had thirty sons, but thirty daughters as well. And then there was Abdon ben Hillel the Pirathonite who had forty sons and thirty grandsons who rode on seventy jackasses.

Why these obscure heros speak to me, I don't know. But somehow, over time and space, they reach out to me and inspire me to ... what? Not to father sixty children like Ibzan of Bethlehem nor to learn to kill people with an oxgoad like Shamgar ben Anat. But even if I can't say exactly what it is they inspire me to do, they do inspire me, sentinels from the hoariest antiquity greeting a rabbi and inspiring him to keep up their work by trying to keep their descendants (and his own) from disappearing forever.

23. Seeing is Believing

Of all the unsung heros of Jewish history, I think Michayahu ben Yimlah is the most regrettably un-famous. Never heard of him? I wouldn't worry about it — almost no one else has either. But he wasn't just no one at all. Michayahu ben Yimlah was, as far as I can determine, the first Jew to claim to have seen God. Not in a dream. And not in a cloud of smoke and lightning. And not from the back, as Scripture says of Moses.

Scripture is actually rather equivocal about Moses. One the one hand, he was celebrated (posthumously, when he couldn't object) as the one Israelite who actually had known God face to face. On the other hand, when Moses asks to be rewarded for his efforts on behalf of Israel by being allowed to gaze on the godhead, God responds mysteriously, agreeing in principle, but pointing out that no human being can see God's face and live. Surprisingly, however, this does not appear to apply to the divine back and so God proposes a compromise. God Himself will place Moses in a cleft within a nearby rock and shield him with His hand until He has passed by. Then God will remove His hand and allow Moses to see His back receding into the distance. How these apparently contradictory traditions fit together historically is not all that clear, but the more profound lesson we learn from contemplating them derives from just that fact — that they *don't* fit together. In other words, there must have been conflicting schools of thought in ancient Israel, one that taught that the greatest experience of communion with God was the opportunity actually to gaze upon His august countenance (an experience that could hardly be denied to Moses, the greatest of all prophets) and another school that believed that the grandeur of God precluded any possibility of gazing upon His form *even* for the greatest prophets. Even Moses, this school would have proposed, was forbidden to look directly at the divine countenance and was forced to look longingly at His receding back — and this was only said because Moses was considered to be the *greatest* of the prophets who needed to be set aside from the others in a way that confirmed the superiority of his prophetic experience. Ordinary prophets, presumably, were to be content with hearing and proclaiming the word of God. The rest of us, I suppose, were to be content with hearing the word of God proclaimed to us by prophets who somehow perceived whatever it was God wished them to communicate to us.

Back to Michayahu ben Yimlah. He wasn't famous, even in antiquity. The rabbis didn't make much of him. The fathers of the Church didn't make much of him. He didn't make much of an impact on the authors of the other books of the Bible either, for that matter — he is mentioned only in the brief passages that tell his specific story and then never referred to again.

But Michayahu ben Yimlah wasn't a nobody, except perhaps after the fact. He was the first person in the extra-Pentateuchal history of Israel to claim to have seen God.

Michayahu was a contemporary of Elijah's and is portrayed in Scripture in one single role, as mediator in a dispute between King Ahab of the northern kingdom of Israel and King Jehoshaphat of Judah in the south. The former is trying to enlist the aid of the latter in a proposed war against the kingdom of Aram over the city of Ramot Gilead which the king of Aram has seized from Ahab. King Jehoshaphat is not interested in taking any chances — he agrees to fight, but he asks for an oracle of confirmation. King Ahab musters up about four hundred prophets and puts the question to them, "Shall I go up against Ramot Gilead or shall I desist?" and their answer is swift and to the point: "Go against it, for God shall deliver it into the hand of the king."

Perhaps it is the immediacy of the reply or perhaps it is the almost startling unanimity of the four hundred, but for whatever reason, Jehoshaphat requires a second opinion and asks if there might be another prophet present through whom the oracle might be confirmed.

Reluctantly, insisting that the one remaining prophet in the palace is a hostile character who generally has only doom to forecast for his king "who loathes him", Ahab produces Michayahu ben Yimlah who, no doubt to Ahab's amazement, offers a prophecy no less encouraging than the other prophets. But just as Jehoshaphat did not find himself able to accept the word of the four hundred at face value, so does Ahab now find himself unable to accept the prophetic encouragement of Michayahu:

And the king said to Michayahu, "How many times do I have to adjure you to speak only truth to me in the name of the Lord?" And he replied, "I see Israel scattered on the mountains like so many sheep without a shepherd. The Lord said, "They have no masters! Let each man return to his home in peace." The King of Israel then said to Jehoshaphat, "Did I not say to you that he would not prophesy good for me, but rather evil?" Michayahu then said, "Therefore hear the word of the Lord. I have seen the Lord seated on His throne and the entire heavenly host standing in attendance, some to the right and some to the left."

The story goes on to explain that Michayahu learned in heaven that the prophetic spirit stimulating the four hundred was a false one sent by God Himself to fool King Ahab into going forth into a battle he would not be able to win. Ahab, naturally, ignores this information, goes up against Ramot Gilead and is killed.

In some ways, this is a typical story of ancient Israel, but what sets it apart is that Michayahu is the first historically datable personality to claim to have seen the God of Israel. The word the text uses for "to see" is the stark, uncompromising Hebrew *ra'iti*, unambiguous and frank. The name used to refer to the Lord is the ineffable, personal name of God, leaving no room for misunderstanding or confusion. No wonder the author of Moses' death notice felt the need to ignore the story of Moses gazing on the back of God and to emphasize that Moses had known God face to face. Certainly Moses, the greatest of all the prophets of ancient Israel, could not be portrayed as having had a less profound prophetic experience of God than the obscure, half-forgotten prophetic nobody, Michayahu ben Yimlah!

Michayahu, about whom nothing at all is known outside the story I've just recounted, had many successors who claimed to have gazed on God. In the middle of the eighth century, for example, we read of a similar experience that befell Isaiah at his prophetic investiture. There the imagery is even richer as the author describes the panoply of celestial beings that surround the divine throne as well as the divine image seated upon it. And there were others, Ezekiel and at least one of the authors of the Book of Daniel among them, other individuals who took up the cudgel in subsequent generations and sought an experience of God that was visual rather than merely aural. I suppose that whether a prophet had visual or aural prophetic experiences depended on whether his own prior conception of God could allow either or both experiences: those prophets who lived within the Biblical tradition of an anthropomorphic godhead were able to cultivate visual experiences, while those prophets who favoured the equally hoary conception of a formless, unseeable (if not quite invisible) Deity had aural experiences which corresponded to their notion of an intelligent and communicative, but ultimately shapeless God who could be heard but never quite seen. What the precise reasons may have been that brought one prophet to conceive of God in one way and another in the other way is probably a psychological question as much as it is a theological one. Indeed, I'm not even sure *if* the prophets were able to choose one path over the other in a conscious, reasoned way. Moderns, it seems to me, certainly can't.

The point is that those prophets who believed in a God Who exists in a visible, anthropomorphic form had visual experiences, while those who believed in a formless godhead experienced aural, intellectual communion with God. And the proof that both schools of thought existed is present in the pages of Scripture itself. It seems reasonable to assume that those Bible stories which speak of a God Who creates mankind in His image, Who walks in the garden at the cool of day, Who personally announces the birth of Isaac to Abraham and Sarah, Who wrestles with Jacob at Peniel and with Moses in the desert, Whose feet hover just above the elders at Sinai and Whose image Moses sees directly and not in a vision or a dream, were told and retold against the background of prophetic experience that presumed that God could be seen. On the other hand, the equally ancient tales of a God Who speaks from within clouds of fog, Who can be known only through the careful scrutiny of His ways, Who manifests Himself to Abraham as a glowing torch, Who appears to Moses from within a burning bush, Who is presumed to dwell high above the world in a palace in the sky and who appears to Elijah as a still, small voice, were told and retold against a background of prophetic experience that presumed that God could be experienced, felt, understood and even heard, but never seen, not even by the greatest patriarchs and prophets.

We moderns have adopted a convenient compromise between the two traditions: we neither see *nor* hear God. We tell ourselves that it would be blasphemous to imagine what God would look like even if we *were* somehow to reach sufficiently ecstatic heights of communion actually to gaze upon the godhead. But we don't swing into the aural camp either — we're pleased to consider anyone crazy who claims that God *actually* speaks to him and doubly so if the message received has any actual content. The God we have constructed for ourselves is a strangely ephemeral deity: capable of being served, obeyed, worshipped and even, on occasion, sensed, but otherwise silent and invisible, a dark, faint shadow of after-the-fact justification looming protectively behind the rituals of our Jewish lives.

24. Zamzumim, Visigoths and Jews

Let's get back to the Jews and Christians thing. I don't want to beat a dead horse, but the Jews are really the sole surviving element of Western society it's socially acceptable to discriminate against. It isn't a status we much relish.

Every other -ism, you see, is long gone. Racism, for example, is absolutely passé. Even people who may actually harbour racist attitudes have the sense that such attitudes are absolutely unacceptable in society. They may even feel that their prejudices are justifiable, even reasonable, but at least everyone — everyone who doesn't actually belong to the Klan or the Aryan Nations, that is — feels obliged to pretend as though that weren't really the case. This is an enormous advance for society, a great step forward not only for black people themselves, but for North American society as a whole. In the final analysis, what matters isn't so much what people really think as much as it is what they accept as being what they are *supposed* to think. Actual attitudes follow later, once resistance has been worn down by years, even decades, of toeing even the most begrudgingly accepted party line. Eventually, the original prejudice seems archaic and silly and it simply goes away. Witness the rampant, even violent prejudice against the Irish that once characterized vast portions of North American society. Anyone hear someone say lately that they'd move if an Irish family moved in down the block?

Sexism is also out. The place of women in the world has been changed forever by now and that's also for the best, I think. I'm sure there are plenty of people who don't like it and who think that a woman's place really is in the kitchen and the bedroom (with the occasional break for cleaning up her husband's mess in front of the television), but no one has the nerve to say it anymore. No high school counsellors *dis*courage girls from applying to college and quotas setting the place of women in professional schools or in trade unions simply do not exist except in situations where they are intended to *increase* the number of female registrants in a given course of study or particular segment of the workplace. Individuals may not like it, but the basic principle of gender equality has become so pervasive as to be almost a given in the public arena. Also a big advance for society as a whole, not just for women.

Discrimination against the elderly or against children, discrimination against lesbians or homosexuals, discrimination based on religion or creed or colour or country of origin — all forbidden, publicly denounced and formally or informally enshrined as forms of bigotry inimical to the norms of decency that govern a society populated by people of good will.

But anti-Semitism? No problem! People don't even think of discrimination against Jews as a problem. There was a letter in the paper the other day by a woman who simply couldn't *believe* that Jews find it irritating that tax dollars are used (at least in Canada) to underwrite the cost of providing discounted postage to Christians at Christmas time so they can save a few pennies on each Christmas card they send out, a perk extended to no other faith group in the land. Well, that's *exactly* how I feel. You want to celebrate your holiday? Good for you — but don't force me to pay for it. I send out New Year's cards at Rosh Hashanah, but I wouldn't dream of expecting *you* to pay for *them*. And trivial though it may sound, the issue is not unimportant. Because the seeds of religious prejudice are sown in a society *precisely* when governments begin, even in harmless, seemingly benign ways, to discriminate between citizens of different faiths and to treat them differently and unequally.

But it goes deeper than the offensive way public funds are used to pay for Christmas celebrations in both the United States and Canada. And to save you the trouble of asking, yes, I'm quite aware of the fact that there is an *enormous* majority of Christians in both countries.

So what? The strength of any democracy worth the name rests in the willingness of the majority to *resist* using its clout in the voting booth to pass laws that deny others their rights. The German Nazis appear to have won fair and square in 1933, but that hardly gave them the right to carry out their racist policies even if they did have a majority in the Reichstag to enact them into law.

The insensitivity to all minority religions is staggering on every level of public life. In my town there is a monument to the servicemen from our community who were killed during the First and Second World Wars. So far, so good. But the monument is in the shape of a large granite cross and stands on public land in front of the city hall. Now, whenever I mention this, some thoughtful soul almost always points out that the servicemen honoured on the monument probably *were* all Christians, so the cruciform monument is actually *appropriate*. There's no real way to know for sure, but I'm even willing to assume they probably *were* all Christians ... but again, so what? I'm sure they were all white men as well (Richmond was a very homogenous place in those days), but nobody — and I mean *nobody* — would *dream* of mentioning *that* on the monument. It wouldn't even be considered, much less done — and yet formally acknowledging the religion these men are presumed to have had is considered reasonable and right even if it does imply that part of the glory of the glorious dead lies in the religion they (are assumed to have) professed while they were still alive. (If I had given my life for this country, would my name be on that monument? God forbid!) My point is that the men who fell in the wars didn't die because they were (a) white, (b) male or (c) Christian. They died because they were Canadians and, it seems to me, that makes their nationality the only relevant point worth mentioning.

Then there's the public school system, where people think it is reasonable for children to be forced to sing the hymns — and occasionally even to recite the prayers — of one specific religion regardless of whether their families are or aren't adherents of that faith. (I won't even *attempt* to guess how offensive serious Christians must find it to see the reality of their faith dismissed and watered down to the point at which *non*-belief in *any* of the tenets of Christianity is *not* considered a reasonable reason *not* to participate in Christian worship.) And yes, there's also the almost unbelievable amount of public money used to promote the values and ideals of one dominant faith regardless of how marginalized the members of other faiths feel as a result.

Jews seem to have a special problem with all of this. There are plenty of other minority religions well represented in my community, but the adherents of those faiths don't seem to get as worked up as we do about these issues. Indeed, many of them put up Christmas lights on their own homes, thereby making the interfaith waters even muddier and further debasing whatever religious message Christianity might presume to have to offer by suggesting that it isn't even necessary to *be* a Christian to celebrate the birth of Christ.

Maybe we react so violently because we are so terrified of disappearing. There weren't that many of us in the first place. Then the Nazis and their henchmen killed one in every three Jews alive in 1939. Now it's more than half a century later and we are still hemorrhaging from the head and the hip from a variety of internal (and mostly self-inflicted) wounds, any one of which would be more than potent enough to finish off the job within a generation or two and all of which together can only spell complete disaster.

Other nationalities don't seem to share this obsession. I never met an Italian who was seriously worried that the Italians might somehow vanish from the pageant of history. For that matter, I don't think I've ever met anyone except a Jew who was seriously concerned that his people might disappear. I suppose you could say that's because I've been asking the wrong nations — instead of asking Italians, why don't I ask some Visigoths or Zamzumim or Phoenicians how *they* feel about the idea of disappearing? But that's just really my point. We Jews *haven't* disappeared, but we remain obsessed with the issue, convinced that with only slightly less diligence, we might vanish into the mists of history like just about all the other nations that were around when we came onto the scene.

And still we endure. What is the secret to Jewish survival? I don't know, but that might be the problem right there. We're obviously doing something right, but we're not quite sure what it is. So do your worst — send discounted Christmas cards and put up all the cruciform cenotaphs you want — maybe the irritation such insensitivity engenders has its own preservative effect on us. Wouldn't that just serve you all right?

EPILOGUE

I have tried to make this book a work that will provide some insight into Jewish life and ritual for both Jews and non-Jewish readers alike. But now I would like to take this opportunity to address myself to my Jewish readers specifically. Non-Jews may feel free to read ahead anyway, but what I have to say here is about how one Jew sees the state of Judaism and is directed specifically at my Jewish readership. Come on now, don't complain — it will be like hearing a rabbi preach from the pulpit without having to sit through all that endless *davening* first.

Unless there is something we haven't thought of yet, we have done everything conceivable to make Judaism unappealing to the very children upon whose interest, allegiance and devotion the future of Jewish life depends. We have created synagogues that squelch spontaneity and personal input in prayer and ritual, religious movements that pride themselves on the degree to which they have succeeded in closing themselves off from any sort of learning deemed potentially dangerous to the preservation of Jewish life as they already know and like it, and vast, powerful organizations of Jewish individuals which actually encourage their members to remain distant and alienated from the rituals of Jewish piety. The situation in Israel, if anything, is even worse.

We have created a world in which most Jews acquire their Jewish education as children and then can't understand why they lack the eyes with which to see the profundity of Jewish ritual as an adult might. We have created a Jewish world in which no rung on the hierarchal ladder is lower, both in terms of income and prestige, than the one occupied by the religious school teacher and then fail to understand why our children are being taught by housewives and errant Israelis rather than by accomplished pedagogues who have chosen to dedicate their lives and their careers to Jewish education. Even the much vaunted day-school movement is as much a part of the problem as it is part of the solution to the extent that families are often forced to choose between paying tuition to their children's school or paying dues to the synagogue to which they ought to belong. The problem would be alleviated by massive community funding of all Jewish schools, but our Jewish leaders are more devoted to building basketball courts and swimming pools and more and more meeting rooms in which to discuss the problems of Jewish education than they are to finding the means to fund Jewish schools.

As far as education goes, we are living in an era of darkness and very little light. When the rest of the world was having *its* Dark Ages, the Jews were enjoying a period of the greatest intellectual activity and creativity. Now, paradoxically, that the world is in the fullest flower of its Information Age, the Jews are labouring under the dark cloud of ignorance and illiteracy. Books written only a century or two ago for the semi-literate are now studied exclusively in graduate seminars by people hoping to complete doctorates in Jewish Studies. Classic works that inspired generations of Jews to attain ever greater heights of spiritual accomplishment are now considered arcane works and are published, to the extent they are published at all, in limited editions for sale as collector's items. The problem doesn't only touch the laity, either: there are large synagogue communities everywhere served by spiritual leaders for whom these books are as closed off as they are to their benighted congregants. The heroes of Jewish spirituality are uncelebrated, their very names unknown to the great masses of Jewish people. Even in synagogues formally dedicated to the strict observance of the law, rabbis who *could* do differently are reduced to giving classes in the rudiments of Hebrew grammar or in the intricacies of keeping a kosher kitchen.

And now for the really bad news. We are the authors of our own degeneracy, the fashioners of this strangely misshapen Jewish world of deformed values and failed piety to which we all belong. We can blame a lot of non-Jews for the untold suffering our people have experienced, but we have built our own institutions, planned the curricula for our own schools, composed the constitutions for our own societies and established our own synagogue communities. We have chosen to worship a God cast in our own image, one who is commonly assumed to espouse a set of virtues and ideals more reminiscent of the Boy Scouts' oath than of the Torah. We have determined, entirely on our own initiative, that God could not possibly want more of any of us than that we be nice people who share our cookies and don't pollute the environment. We have trashed the fruits of four millennia of spiritual development in favour of a feel-good kind of religion that has as its cardinal virtues the twin goals of fitting into the society around us and not provoking the *goyim* to build more concentration camps.

But it doesn't have to be this way. Each individual Jewish soul has the potential to exist in a state of ongoing, permanent communion with God. And each of us has the potential to participate in the pursuit of the kind of piety that yields the spiritual wealth which is the common patrimony of all Jewish people rather than the kind of ritual-by-rote religion that merely perpetuates itself endlessly without any particular justification for its existence being apparent to the outside observer or inherent in its texture. We have made the commandments of the Torah into little more than Jewish rabbits' feet, talismans of the most basely superstitious nature that we uphold, if we uphold them at all, for fear of what will happen if we jettison them rather than because we expect or even hope that they will lead us to God. Worst of all, we have created a Jewish world in which intense, honest intellectual inquiry into the nature and history of Judaism is deemed inimical to observance and something best renounced by any who would be called traditional. And thus we have Judaism on the threshold of the twenty-first (Christian) century: a house divided against itself in which individual Jews who wish to belong to synagogue communities are expected, indeed required, to choose *either* affiliation with congregations that stress traditional observance but condemn scholarship as blasphemy *or* affiliation with almost totally non-observant communities that have paid for the candour and intellectual honesty of their approach to Judaism with whatever shreds of traditional observance they might otherwise have managed to maintain.

I don't know why millions died during the Holocaust. But I do know, or I think I do, why other millions are being lost to the Jewish people in a less violent, but no less permanent, way. Jews do not drift away from religion because they hate God or because they are possessed of some insane mania to destroy the faith of their own ancestors. They drift away because Judaism is resistible, a tasty snack for people *who like that sort of thing,* but something other people with less refined spiritual appetites can easily do without. The challenge, therefore, is to make Judaism something irresistible, something no sane Jewish people will distance themselves from for fear of losing the opportunity to know God in a way available only to those who live Jewish life to its fullest. The task is overwhelming and is perhaps already beyond our grasp. Still, I continue to feel more noble than foolish as I spend my life harping on these ideas and, at least until the balance shifts, I suppose I shall keep on keeping on. The future looks alternately hopeless and merely bleak to me, but what choice do we have? To truly worship the Redeemer of Israel, Israel can do no less than bring about its own redemption.

Bibliographical Notes

(In the following pages, **BT** is the abbreviation for the Babylonian Talmud and **PT** is the abbreviation for the Palestinian Talmud.)

Chapter 3: The story of Purim is told in the Biblical Book of Esther, where specific reference to the origin of the holiday itself may be found in verses 27-32 of the ninth chapter. The tradition about becoming inebriated on Purim to the point of not knowing the difference between Mordechai and Haman is presented in the name of the Talmudic teacher Rava at **BT** Megillah 7b. The customs of giving charity to the poor, sending gifts of food to others and feasting on Purim have their Biblical basis at Esther 9:22 and are elaborated and codified in the "Orakh Chayyim" section of the *Shulchan Arukh*, chapters 694 and 695.

Chapter 5: The laws of the Nazirite are discussed in the sixth chapter of the Book of Numbers. Rabbi Eliezer Hakappar's teaching is preserved in the Talmud at **BT** Nazir 19a. (An alternate view of that same rabbi's is preserved elsewhere in the same tractate.) Rabbi Akiba calls vows "a fence around asceticism" in *The Ethics of the Fathers* 3:17. Rabbi Meir's teaching about Adam is at **BT** Eruvin 18b. The story about King David and the ten concubines is found in the Bible at the beginning of the twentieth chapter of 2 Samuel. Rabbi Yochanan's interpretation of that story is preserved at **PT** Sanhedrin 2:3, 20a.

Chapter 6: The rabbis' remark that it is better to perform a religious act for the wrong reasons than not to do it at all is taken from a remark of the talmudic teacher Rav taught by his pupil Rabbi Judah and preserved at **BT** Pesachim 50b and half a dozen other locations in the Talmud.

Chapter 7: The dietary laws appear in two great clusters in the Torah, in the eleventh chapter of Leviticus and the fourteenth chapter of Deuteronomy. The prohibition of mixing dairy and meat products in the same dish or at the same meal is the rabbinic interpretation of the Biblical prohibition of seething a kid in its mother's milk repeated three times in Scripture, in the twenty-third and thirty-fourth chapters of Exodus and the fourteenth chapter of Deuteronomy. The word "kosher" (in its Hebrew form, *kasher*) appears in the Bible only at Esther 8:5.

Chapter 8: The remark that no mortal may behold God and live is found at Exodus 33:20. The parable of the mirror is found in an ancient text called *The Visions of Ezekiel*, published by Ithamar Gruenwald in *Temirin*, ed. I. Weinstock (Jerusalem, 1972), vol. 1, pp. 101-140. The Bible reports that Moses saw God face to face at Deuteronomy 34:10.

Chapter 9: The Talmudic justification for observing two days of the festivals is found at **BT** Betzah 4b. The Biblical verse that serves as the Scriptural justification for reciting the Grace after Meals is Deuteronomy 8:10. The five-word grace is cited in the Talmud in the name of the unlearned Benjamin the Shepherd at **BT** Brachot 40b, where the view is expressed (and challenged) that the great Talmudic teacher Rav accepted it is a valid version of the grace. The Talmud refers to the old Palestinian custom of reading the Torah over a three-year cycle at **BT** Megillah 29b.

Chapter 10: "Let the waters bring forth swarms of living creatures" is taken from Genesis 1:20. The two largest lists of sexual prohibitions in Scripture are the eighteenth and twentieth chapters of Leviticus. Some of the material in this chapter is taken from the opening chapter of my 1992 novel *The Truth About Marvin Kalish*.

Chapter 12: *Kol Nidre* is the first prayer recited in synagogue on the eve of Yom Kippur and, by extension, the name popularly used to refer to the whole service. The prayer that speaks of the Jews passing one by one like sheep before their Shepherd is the famous *Unetaneh Tokef* prayer attributed to Rabbi Amnon of medieval Mainz. The custom of tossing bread crumbs into a stream as a way of stimulating oneself to cast off one's sins is called Tashlich and has its origins in a literalist approach to Micah 7:19. The tradition that Rosh Hashanah is the anniversary of the creation of the world is an ancient one recorded in the Talmud at **BT** Rosh Hashanah 8a, 10b and 27a and at Avodah Zarah 8a in the name of Rabbi Eliezer.

Chapter Fourteen: *Matzah* is called the bread of affliction that the Israelites ate as slaves in Egypt in one of the most prominent liturgical sections of the Haggadah recited on the eve of Passover. Although the phrase "bread of affliction" is indeed found at Deuteronomy 16:3, the context there seems to suggest that that passage, like the earlier reference at Exodus 12:39, presumes that *matzah* is to be eaten at Passover in recollection of the fact that the Israelites' alacrity in obeying God's command to leave Egypt was so great that they didn't even wait for their dough to rise. They took it along with them and baked it unrisen and *matzah* crackers were the result.

Chapter 15: The phrase acknowledging God as He who causes evening to fall is taken from the first benediction preceding the *Hear, O Israel* confession of faith in the regular weekday and Sabbath evening liturgy and may be found in any traditional prayerbook. The rabbinic dictum according to which God may only be found in that which is hidden from the eye is a recurring theme in all my books and may be found in the Talmud at **BT** Baba Metzia 42a in the name of Rabbi Isaac. *Davening* is the Yiddish term for prayer used regularly in the English speech of North American Jews. The phrase "In Your light, we see light" comes from Psalms 36:10. *What the Moon Brought* was written by Sadie R. Weilerstein and was originally published in 1942. It remains available through the Jewish Publication Society in Philadelphia.

Chapter 16: This chapter is based on some ideas I published in *Conservative Judaism* 44:3(1992), pp. 3-15. God is described as wearing light as a garment at Psalms 104:2. *Tallis* and *tallit* are the same word, the former being the Yiddish form that has entered the English speech of many North American Jews and the latter, the word pronounced according to the Sephardic, now the Israeli, rules of Hebrew pronunciation.

Chapter 17: *The High Ways to Perfection* by Abraham Maimuni was published in S. Rosenblatt's translation in Baltimore in 1938. The song of Shantideva is published in Edward Conze's translation in his *Buddhist Scriptures* (Middlesex, Baltimore and Victoria [Australia], 1959), pp. 100-102. The closing parable is from the fictitious *Midrash Eli Melekh*, a book I have been writing for several years for Rabbi

Elimelech Weissbrot.

Chapter 18: The original story about Moses and Zipporah appears in Exodus 4:24-26. Its midrashic amplification and elucidation appears in several places in rabbinic literature, most notably at Exodus Rabbah 5:8 and at BT Nedarim 32b (where it is Moses' foot that is euphemistically said to have been hanging out of the snake's mouth!). I have taken a number of liberties with the rabbinic sources in my retelling and fleshing-out of the story. The reader might also wish to take note of the fact that a tradition to the effect that Moses was born already circumcised (i.e. foreskinless) is recorded in the name of some unidentified "others" at BT Sotah 12a and that, on the very next page of Talmud, Rabbi Yossi ben Chaninah suggests that Pharaoh's daughter was able to recognize Moses as a Hebrew child when she found him afloat in the Nile specifically because she saw that he was circumcised (or at least that he looked *as though* he had been circumcised). The rabbi who thinks Zipporah was referring to her son when she utters her mysterious remark about the bridegroom is an unidentified rabbi of the mishnaic period whose opinion is preserved at PT Nedarim 3:14, 38b. *Bris* is the Yiddish/Hebrew term for circumcision in common use in the English speech of North American Jews.

Chapter 21: The sources for the Chanukah story are found, mostly, among the post-Biblical Jewish books preserved in Greek, the so-called Books of the Apocrypha. The First Book of Maccabees, for example, was probably written in Hebrew by a near-contemporary to the events described (the latest events in the book date to c. 135 B.C.E., around thirty years later). The Second Book of Maccabees is a synopsis of a lost five-volume work by the otherwise unknown Jason of Cyrene and only covers the actual events involving the Maccabees and their enemies in Jerusalem in the fourth decade of the second century B.C.E. My understanding of the events is based heavily on the first chapters of the Second Book of Maccabees. The Biblical Book of Daniel also has a large number of highly esoteric references to the Maccabees and their activities, especially in chapters eight and eleven. Other references can be found in the works of Josephus, Diodorus, Tacitus and certain Byzantine historians, especially John Malalas.

Chapter 22: The story of Ehud ben Gera is told at Judges 3:15-30. (In the Bible, Eglon rises from his privy stool when told that the message Ehud is bearing him is a message from God, but that's not the way I see it in my dream.) Shamgar ben Anat is mentioned at Judges 3:31. The Biblical notice about Yair the Gileadite is at Judges 10:3-5. Tola ben Puah is mentioned at Judges 10:1-2; Ibzan of Bethlehem, at Judges 12:8-10. The reference to Abdon ben Hillel is at Judges 12:13-15.

Chapter 23: Moses is said to have known God face to face at Deuteronomy 34:10. At Numbers 12:8, God is specifically heard to say that He allows Moses to gaze at his image. Still, when Scripture tells of God and Moses speaking with each other at the Tent of Meeting, a special tent in which such social intercourse between the divine and terrestrial realms was deemed possible, it is always in a pillar of cloud that God appears. Perhaps we are to suppose that it was during his famous forty-day sojourn on Mount Sinai that God appeared in his (presumably anthropomorphic) splendour to Moses, but Scripture does not say that in so many words. The story about how Moses specifically asked to gaze upon the godhead only to be allowed to peer out at God's back as He passed by is found at Exodus 33:17-23. The story of Michayahu is told in the twenty-second chapter of 2 Kings and then retold in the eighteenth chapter of 2 Chronicles. Michayahu should not be confused with the prophet Micah, although they have different versions of the same name, as is obvious from a comparison of 1 Kings 22:15 with 2 Chronicles 18:14. (The canonical prophet Micah lived later on, during the reigns of Kings Jotham, Ahaz and Hezekiah of Judah.) The story of Isaiah's prophetic investiture is told at Isaiah 6:1-13. The story of Ezekiel's experience of the visually accessible godhead is found in the first and tenth chapters of his book; the similar, yet different experiences of the author (or, more probably, one of the authors) of Daniel may be found in the seventh chapter of that Biblical book.